THE COMPLETE BOOK OF OFFENSIVE FOOTBALL DRILLS

Jerry Tolley

Former Head Football Coach
Elon University

ISBN: 1-58518-935-9
Library of Congress Control Number: 2005926719

Cover design: Jeanne Hamilton
Book layout: Jeanne Hamilton
Diagrams: Deborah Oldenburg
Front cover photo: Streeter Lecka/Getty Images

Coaches Choice
P.O. Box 1828
Monterey, CA 93942
www.coacheschoice.com

Dedication

It has been an honor and a privilege to have been associated with many outstanding football coaches. Three of these coaches have had a significant impact on my personal coaching career. It is because of their influence that I dedicate this book in their honor.

Shirley S. "Red" Wilson

Coach S. S. "Red" Wilson was my college coaching mentor. I first served with Coach Wilson for one year at Fayetteville Senior High in Fayetteville, North Carolina, and again for ten years at Elon College (now Elon University) in Elon, North Carolina. Coach Wilson was a remarkable football coaching legend, proving his coaching abilities in high school, small college at Elon, and later at Division I Duke University. In the high school arena, he captured two North Carolina AAAA titles at R. J. Reynolds High School. At Elon, he led the Fighting Christians to six conference titles and participated in the NAIA national playoffs on three different occasions, advancing to the championship game in 1973. As head coach at Duke, he coached the Blue Devils to back-to-back winning seasons in 1981 and 1982, the first in twenty years.

From Coach Wilson I learned three very important lessons. The first was the importance of motivation in building a championship program. Highly motivated teams win games and uninspired teams don't. Secondly, he taught me that organization was the cornerstone of every successful football program. And finally, Coach Wilson taught me that building loyalty among the coaching staff, the players, the administration, and the fans was imperative.

Clarence Stasavich
(February 9, 1913 – October 24, 1974)

Clarence Stasavich was my college coach at East Carolina University. I was also honored to serve under him as a Pirate graduate assistant. Coach "Stas" was truly a college football coaching legend. A member of a number of football Halls-of-Fame, he was named National College Coach of the Year in 1959 at Lenoir Rhyne College and again at East Carolina University in 1964. Before arriving at East Carolina in 1962, he gained much notoriety at Lenoir Rhyne in Hickory, North Carolina, leading the Bears to numerous conference titles and the NAIA National Championship in 1960. On the ECU campus, he led the Pirates to three consecutives bowl victories, including Tangerine Bowl wins in 1964 and 1965. He also served as athletic director.

From "Stas" I learned the importance of planning and putting an operational system in place. He also taught me that teaching the basic fundamentals through well-defined football drills was the hallmark for establishing a winning football program.

William D. "Bill" Billings

William D. "Bill" Billings was my high school coach at John A. Holmes High in Edenton, NC. Under his leadership, the Aces from Holmes High won four state football titles in 1954, 1956, 1957, and 1960. Later at Middletown High School in Middletown, Delaware, he captured mythical State titles in 1964, 1965, 1966, and 1970. Overall he compiled a record of 223-51-9 and once led his Middletown team on a fifty-three-game winning streak.

It was from Coach Billings that I first developed a love for the game. He taught me that through hard work and dedication all things are possible. Coach Billings was a great competitor and one of the all-time great high school coaching legends.

I was honored and privileged to have played for and/or coached under each of these outstanding coaching legends. For this I will be eternally grateful.

Acknowledgments

Sincere appreciation is expressed to the many outstanding coaches who have contributed offensive drills to this book. Their commitment to the time-honored tradition of sharing ideas among the coaching fraternity made the editorship of this publication both an honor and a privilege.*

Gratitude is expressed to Kristin Simonetti, a student at Elon University, for her editorial assistance and masterful job of typing the manuscript. Also thanked is Pat Whelan for her administrative support.

A loving appreciation is expressed to my wonderful wife, Joanie, for her patience, understanding, and support.

*Special appreciation is extended to each of the contributing coaches who assisted in the verification of all compiled biographical information for accuracy. It should be noted that all biographical information reflects only that which had occurred before September 1, 2004.

Foreword

As a head coach, I believe in scoring points and winning football games. It is my pleasure to introduce Jerry Tolley's newest football drill book, *The Complete Book of Offensive Football Drills*. Dr. Tolley, a former National Coach of the Year, led his Elon University team to back-to-back national titles in 1980 and 1981.

A noted author, Jerry's other drill books include *The American Football Coaches Guidebook To Championship Football Drills, 101 Winning Football Drills From The Legends of The Game*, and *The Complete Book of Defensive Football Drills*.

Dr. Tolley's latest publication, *The Complete Book of Offensive Football Drills*, is one that I consider to be an offensive coach's dream. The book is expertly organized by position and purpose. It contains drills for running backs, quarterbacks, centers and other linemen, tight ends, and wide receivers, as well as drills for teaching the passing game and the option offense.

In all, the book contains more than 140 specific offensive football drills featuring such outstanding coaches as Phil Fulmer, Joe Paterno, Dennis Franchione, Ken Hatfield, Steve Spurrier, LaVell Edwards, George O'Leary, Billy Joe, Fisher DeBerry, and many others.

This comprehensive practical drill book has application for every football coach and at every level of play. I enthusiastically recommend it to the coaching profession.

Bobby Bowden
Head Coach
Florida State University

Contents

Running Back Drills

BAG DRILL*

John H. McKay (Deceased)
University of Oregon, University of Southern California, Tampa Bay Buccaneers
National Champions: Southern California 1962, 1967, 1972, and 1974
National Coach of the Year: Southern California 1962 and 1972
College Football Hall of Fame: 1988
AFCA President: 1973

Objective: To teach and practice the proper fundamentals and techniques of running the football. Incorporated are skills related to receiving a handoff, cutting, protecting the football, power, balance, and ball awareness.

Equipment Needed: One large blocking dummy, three hand shields, and footballs

Description:

- Position a player holding a large blocking dummy on a selected line of scrimmage. Two additional players with hand shields are placed side-by-side and five-yards behind the front dummy holder. A fourth player holding a hand shield is positioned another five-yards downfield (see diagram).

- Running backs line up in a straight line five-yards behind the large blocking dummy.

- The coach is positioned in a dive relationship to the row of running backs.

- On coach's cadence and snap count, the first running back drives from his stance and receives the handoff.

- As the runner approaches the first blocking dummy, the player holding that dummy tilts it either left or right. The ballcarrier breaks the opposite way of the tilted dummy and sprints to the defenders holding the hand shields.

- He now blasts through the hand shields as the defenders *jam* him and try to prevent his progress.

- The ballcarrier now sprints past the final shield holder as that defender throws the shield at the runner's feet. The ballcarrier executes a high step to avoid tripping or falling.

- The drill continues until all running backs have had a sufficient number of repetitions.

- The handoffs should be executed both left and right.

---

*Reprinted with permission from 101 Winning Football Drills: From the Legends of the Game by Jerry Toley

Coaching Points:

- Always check to see that running backs are aligned correctly and are in their proper stances.

- Instruct running backs to keep their eyes straight-ahead and focused on the blocking dummy as they receive the handoff.

- Make sure that running backs' shoulders are low and squared to the defenders as they explode through the collision area.

- Instruct runners to kick through the thrown dummy to simulate breaking a tackle.

- Insist that the drill be conducted at full speed.

Safety Considerations:

- Proper warm-up should precede the drill.

- Instruct the defenders in the collision area not to be abusive as they *jam* the ballcarrier.

Variation:

- Can be used with or without any one of the dummy or hand-shield areas.

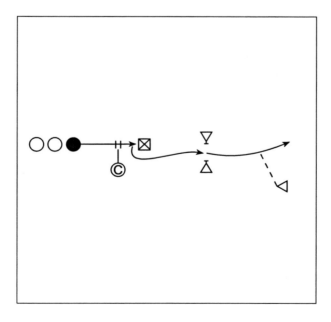

CORNER DRILL

Dick Sheridan
Furman University, North Carolina State University

Objective: To teach and practice the proper fundamentals and techniques of open-field running.

Equipment Needed: Footballs

Description:

- Align a row of running backs on a selected hash mark at the plus-20-yard line.
- Position a row of tacklers in a corresponding relationship on the minus-10-yard line.
- The coach, holding a football, is positioned on the 15-yard line.
- On command, the coach pitches the football to the first ballcarrier who avoids the *position* tackle of the defender and sprints for the goal line. The boundaries of the drill are set as the hash marks and near sideline (see diagram).
- Drill continues until all running backs have had a sufficient number of repetitions.
- Drill should be conducted from both the left and right hash marks.

Coaching Points:

- Make sure running backs use the desired tackle avoidance techniques (head fake, cutback, change of pace, stiff arm, etc.).
- Instruct running backs to carry the football correctly and under the outside arm.
- Insist that the running backs always run toward the goal line.

Safety Considerations:

- Proper warm-up should precede drill.
- Drill area (including sideline areas) should be clear of all foreign articles.
- Instruct the defenders that this is a *position* tackling drill and not a live tackling drill.

Variations:

- Can be used as a tight end and wide receiver drill.
- Can be used as a defensive tackling drill.
- Can be used as a live tackling drill.

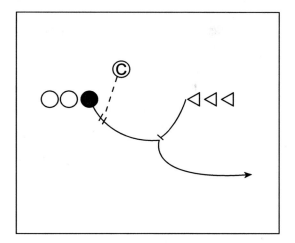

BARREL RUN*

Grant G. Teaff
Texas Tech University, McMurry University, Angelo State University, Baylor University
National Coach of the Year: Baylor 1974
College Football Hall of Fame: 2001
AFCA Executive Director: 1994-present

Objective: To teach and practice the proper fundamentals and techniques of running the football. Incorporated are skills related to reading, protecting the football, quickness, reaction, balance, and explosion.

Equipment Needed: Five large barrels, three large blocking dummies, and footballs

Description:

- Place five barrels two-feet apart as shown in the diagram.

- Position two defenders behind the back two barrels with instructions to grab for the football as a ballcarrier comes by.

- Place three large blocking dummies with a holder in a triangular alignment three-yards behind the barrel area. Two yards separate the three dummies.

- Align a row of ballcarriers five yards in front of the drill area.

- The coach is positioned behind the middle barrel.

- On command, the first ballcarrier drives from his stance and sprints between the first two barrels as the coach appears from behind either side of the middle barrel.

- The ballcarrier now cuts in the opposite direction and moves up and around the middle barrel.

- As the runner sprints between the back two barrels, the defenders positioned behind them reach out and try to pull the football away from the ballcarrier.

- The running back now drives into the middle standup dummy and spins out either left or right. He then cuts off the back dummy according to the way the dummy is tilted by the holder.

- The drill continues until all the running backs have had a sufficient number of repetitions.

*Reprinted with permission from 101 Winning Football Drills: From the Legends of the Game by Jerry Tolley

Coaching Points:

- Always check to see that the running backs are aligned correctly and are in their proper stances.

- Always stress the importance of carrying the football properly.

- Instruct the running backs to use a lateral step when breaking away from the movement of the coach from behind the middle barrel.

- Insist that all running backs keep their heads up throughout the entire drill.

- Insist that the drill be conducted at full speed.

Safety Considerations:

- Proper warm-up should precede the drill.

- Helmets should always be worn with chinstraps snapped.

- Check barrels regularly to make sure they are free of sharp edges.

Variation:

- Can be used with various dummy alignments and running back movements in finishing the drill.

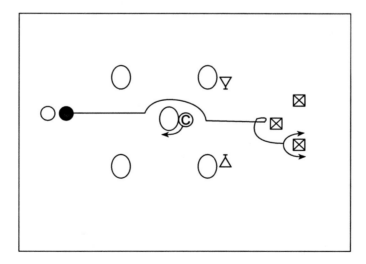

DIVE ACTION PASS DRILL

Vernon Fewell

Sul Ross State University, Texas Lutheran College, University Mary Hardin-Baylor

Objective: To teach and practice the proper fundamentals and techniques of reading the blitz and reacting accordingly.

Equipment Needed: Two blocking dummies and two footballs

Description:

- Align a center, quarterback, and running back over the football on a selected line of scrimmage.
- Position a linebacker and free safety in their regular alignment over the offense.
- Place a blocking dummy at the offensive guard and tackle positions to form a running alley.
- The coach is positioned behind the offense and indicates the pass pattern to be run. He also signals the linebacker to either blitz, drop to hook zone, or play man-to-man on the running back.
- On quarterback's cadence and ball snap, the running back reads the linebacker. If the linebacker blitzes, the running back stays in and blocks (see diagram). If the linebacker drops to the *hook* zone, the running back sprints downfield and tries to outrun the free safety. If he cannot get behind the safety, he *cuts* inside of him (see diagram). If the linebacker *locks on* man-to-man, the running back outruns the linebacker to the goal line (see diagram).
- Drill continues until all personnel have had a sufficient number of repetitions.
- Drill should be conducted both left and right and from various field positions.

Coaching Points:

- Always check to see that all personnel are aligned correctly and are in their proper stances.
- Instruct the running backs always to assume the linebacker will blitz.
- Insist that all running backs set up properly and execute their pass block correctly.
- Instruct the running backs to release for a pass only if the linebacker does not blitz.

Safety Considerations:

- Proper warm-up should precede drill.
- Drill area should be clear of all foreign articles.

- The drill should progress from formwork to live work.
- The coach should monitor closely the intensity of the drill.
- Instruct the running backs never to *cut block* the linebacker.
- Instruct the linebackers and free safeties never to tackle or break through the receiver for the football.

Variations:

- Can be used with varying linebacker alignments.
- Can be used with linebackers holding a hand shield.
- Can be used as a linebacker and free safety drill.

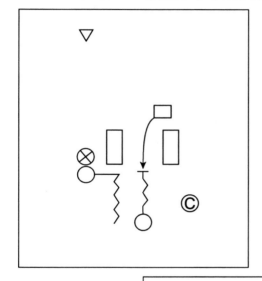

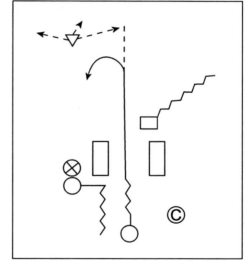

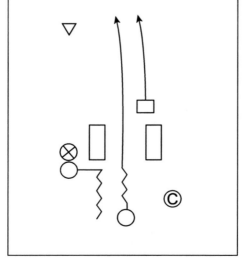

BLAST DRILL*

Robert "Bob" Devaney (Deceased)
Michigan State University, University of Wyoming, University of Nebraska
National Champions: Nebraska 1970 and 1971
National Coach of the Year: Nebraska 1971
College Football Hall of Fame: 1981
Amos Alonzo Stagg Award: 1994

Objective: To teach and practice the proper fundamentals and techniques of running the football. Incorporated are skills related to receiving a handoff, tackle avoidance, balance, and carrying and protecting the football.

Equipment Needed: Three large blocking dummies and footballs

Description:

- Position two players holding large blocking dummies one-yard apart on a selected line of scrimmage. A third dummy is held three-yards behind the players holding the front two dummies.

- A quarterback is aligned one yard in front of either of the two front-held dummies and in a dive relationship to a row of running backs (see diagram).

- On the quarterback's cadence and snap count, the first running back drives from his stance and receives the handoff.

- He now *blasts* through the collision area as the two dummy holders *jam* him and try to prevent his progress.

- The ballcarrier continues his run and drives into the third dummy and then spins off either left or right and sprints for a designated distance.

- The drill continues until all running backs have had a sufficient number of repetitions.

- The handoffs should be executed both left and right.

*Reprinted with permission from 101 Winning Football Drills: From the Legends of the Game by Jerry Tolley

Coaching Points:

- Always check to see that running backs are aligned correctly and are in their proper stances.

- Instruct the running backs to focus their eyes straight ahead as they receive the handoff.

- Insist that the drill be conducted at full speed.

Safety Considerations:

- Proper warm-up should precede the drill.

- Instruct the defenders in the collision area not to be too aggressive as they *jam* the ballcarrier.

Variation:

- Can be used with various running-back movements in attacking the final dummy (stiff arm, sidestep, etc.).

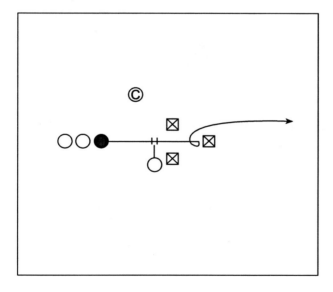

FLAG DRILL

Douglas T. "Doug" Porter
Fort Valley State College, Howard University, Grambling State University,
Mississippi Valley State College, Xavier University-Louisiana

Objective: To teach and practice the proper fundamentals and techniques of running the football with special emphasis on staying inbounds.

Equipment Needed: Four hand shields and footballs

Description:

- Position four defenders holding hand shields four yards apart on an angle from the 12-yard line to the goal line. The defender on the 12-yard line stands four yards from the sideline while the defender on the goal line is placed only six inches from the sideline (see diagram).
- Align a row of running backs on the 20-yard line at the near hash mark.
- The coach, with football in hand, stands in a quarterback relationship to the row of running backs.
- On cadence and snap count, the coach pitches the football to the first running back, who runs for the near corner of the end zone.
- As the runner approaches the shield area, he lowers his shoulders and strives to stay inbounds as the four shield holders, in turn, try to force him out of bounds.
- Drill continues until all running backs have had a sufficient number of repetitions.
- Drill should be conducted from both the left and right hash marks.

Coaching Points:

- Always check to see that running backs are aligned correctly and are in their proper stances.
- Insist that running backs carry the football under the outside arm.
- Instruct running backs to maintain a low forward body lean and to meet each defender with a good forearm-shoulder blow.

Safety Considerations:

- It is imperative that proper warm-up precede drill.

- Drill area (including sideline areas) should be clear of all foreign articles.

- Instruct shield holders not to abuse the running backs and not to *jam* them in the head area.

Variations:

- Can be used with a varying number of shield holders.

- Can be used with different backfield actions.

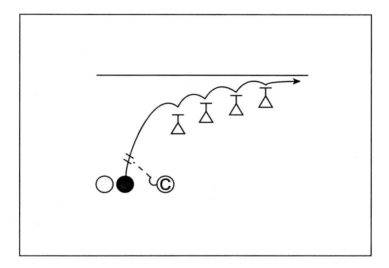

CADENCE AND HANDOFF*

Dave Maurer
Wittenberg University
National Champions: 1973 and 1975
National Coach of the Year: 1973 and 1975
College Football Hall of Fame: 1991
AFCA President: 1984

Objective: To teach and practice the proper fundamentals and techniques in executing the handoff. Special emphasis is placed on cadence recognition.

Equipment Needed: Eight large blocking dummies and footballs

Description:

- Lay two rows of four blocking dummies seven-feet apart. A three-yard separation is between each dummy (see diagram).

- Position a quarterback holding a football one-yard back and to the outside of the first dummy on each side.

- Align a row of running backs behind each row of dummies and in a dive relationship to the quarterback.

- The coach stands at the end of, and in between, the two rows of dummies. He designates different quarterbacks to call cadence.

- On designated quarterback's cadence and snap count, both quarterbacks execute the dive handoffs to their respective running back.

- After receiving the handoff, the running backs run over and through the dummies. Running backs are instructed to change lines after each repetition.

- The drill continues until all drill participants have had a sufficient number of repetitions.

Coaching Points:

- Check to see that all personnel are aligned correctly and are in their proper stances.

- Instruct the quarterbacks to call their cadence with authority.

*Reprinted with permission from *101 Winning Football Drills: From the Legends of the Game* by Jerry Tolley

- Make sure that quarterback *feathers* the football on the running back's *belt buckle* and that he rides the ballcarrier after the ball exchange has been executed.

- Instruct running backs to anticipate the snap count, form good pockets for receiving the football, and focus their eyes straight ahead.

Safety Considerations:

- Proper warm-up should precede the drill.

- Helmets should be worn with chinstraps snapped.

Variations:

- Can incorporate centers.

- Can be used with coach flashing fingers and with running backs calling out the correct numbers to ensure that ballcarriers are focusing on the point of attack.

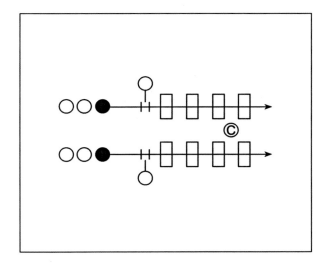

FLARE PASS DRILL

Gerry Faust
University of Notre Dame, University of Akron

Objective: To teach and practice the proper fundamentals and techniques of catching a *flare* pass under the threat of contact.

Equipment Needed: Hand shield and footballs

Description:

- Align a center, quarterback, and running back over the football on a selected line of scrimmage.
- Other drill participants stand adjacent to the drill area.
- The coach, holding a football, stands in the *flare* pass reception area with a hand shield.
- On cadence and ball snap quarterback executes his assigned pass drop as the running back runs his designated *flare* pass route.
- As the running back catches the pass thrown by the quarterback, the coach *jams* the receiver with the hand shield.
- Drill continues until all running backs have had a sufficient number of repetitions.
- Drill should be conducted to both the left and the right and from various field positions.

Coaching Points:

- Always check to see that all personnel are aligned correctly and are on their proper stances.
- Insist that the running backs run their *flare* pass patterns correctly.
- Always emphasize the importance of concentration.

Safety Considerations:

- Proper warm-up should precede drill.
- Drill area should be clear of all foreign articles.
- The coach should never *jam* the running back in the head area.

Variations:

- Can be used with various running back pass patterns.
- Can be used with the coach varying the timing of his *jamming* of the running backs.
- Can be used as a tight end or wide receiver drill.

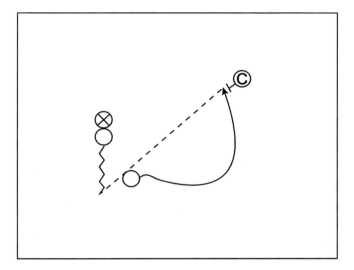

GAUNTLET

Walter A. Barr
Shepherd College, Shenandoah University

Objective: To teach and practice the proper fundamentals and techniques of receiving a hand off, protecting the football, and open field running.

Equipment Needed: Eight cones and footballs

Description:

- Form a gauntlet by aligning two rows of running backs one yard apart and perpendicular to a selected line of scrimmage.

- Position a quarterback, holding a football, and a running back in a proper dive relationship to the gauntlet (see diagram). Gauntlet personnel rotate to the running back position.

- An area 15 yards by 25 yards is defined behind the gauntlet using eight cones (see diagram).

- A defender is positioned 10 yards behind the gauntlet.

- On cadence and snap count, the running back drives from his stance and receives the handoff from the quarterback. He then runs the gauntlet as the gauntlet personnel try to *jerk* the football from his hands.

- After the running back clears the gauntlet, he avoids the open field tackle of the defender and runs for the score.

- Drill continues until all personnel have had a sufficient number of repetitions.

- Drill should be conducted from both left and right handoff alignments.

Coaching Points:

- Always check to see that all personnel are aligned correctly and are in their proper stances.

- Encourage running backs to secure the football through the gauntlet area.

- Instruct the running backs to run under control in the open field and to emphasize their tackle avoidance techniques as they evade the defender.

Safety Considerations:

- It is imperative that proper warm-up precedes drill.

- Instruct the running backs not to run over the defender.

- Instruct the defensive backs *not* to pursue the running back until after he has cleared the gauntlet area.

- The coach should monitor closely the intensity of the drill.

- A quick whistle is imperative with this drill.

Variation:

- Can be used as an open field tackling drill.

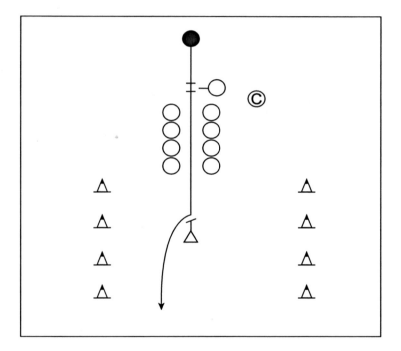

FIGURE-EIGHT DRILL OR MONKEY ROLL*

Richard "Dick" Tomey
Miami University (OH), Northern Illinois University, Davidson College,
University of Kansas, University of California at Los Angeles, San Francisco 49ers,
University of Texas, San Jose State University, University of Hawaii,
University of Arizona

Objective: To teach and practice the proper fundamentals of holding on to the football.

Equipment Needed: Three footballs

Description:

- Position three running backs, each holding a football, two-yards apart on a selected line of scrimmage. Other running backs fall in behind the first three drill participants.

- The coach stands in front of the three lines.

- On the coach's first command, the first three running backs step forward five yards and assume the *football position*. On coach's second command, the drill participants execute the standard figure-eight *monkey roll* as follows:
  - The middle running back hits the ground rolling to his right.
  - The running back positioned to the right of the middle running back dives sideways over the middle running back and rolls to his left.
  - The third running back dives over the second running back and rolls to his right.
  - This procedure continues for seven to eight seconds.

- On the coach's third command, the three running backs stand in place *chopping* their feet.

- On the coach's final command, the three running backs sprint up the field for ten yards.

- The drill continues until all running backs have had a sufficient number of repetitions.

- The drill should be conducted both left and right and with the football tucked under each arm.

*Reprinted with permission from 101 Winning Football Drills: From the Legends of the Game by Jerry Tolley

Coaching Points:

- Insist that all running backs secure the football properly.
- Instruct all running backs to regain their feet after each roll.
- Insist that the drill be conducted at full speed.

Safety Considerations:

- Proper warm-up should precede the drill.
- The drill should progress from half speed to full speed.

Variation:

- Can be used for all ball-handling positions.

GAUNTLET AND ANTI-FUMBLE DRILL

Bobby Collins

Colorado State University, Mississippi State University, George Washington University, Virginia Polytechnic Institute and State University, University of North Carolina, University of Southern Mississippi, Southern Methodist University

Objective: To teach and practice the proper fundamentals and techniques of receiving a handoff, securing the football, and exploding through the line.

Equipment Needed: Three large blocking dummies and footballs

Description:

- Align two defenders holding blocking dummies two feet apart on a selected line of scrimmage.

- Form a gauntlet by aligning two rows of running backs one yard apart behind each of the held dummies.

- Position a row of running backs four yards in front of the drill area.

- A third blocking dummy is held three yards behind the gauntlet area (see diagram).

- Position a quarterback, holding a football, in a dive relationship to the row of running backs. Gauntlet personnel rotate to the running back position.

- On cadence and snap count, the first running back drives from his stance and receives the handoff from the quarterback. He *explodes* through the two held dummies and then runs through the gauntlet of running backs as they try to *jerk* the football from his hands.

- After clearing the gauntlet area, the running back executes a shoulder drive into the third dummy and then either pivots or slides to the outside and runs for the score.

- Drill continues until all running backs have had a sufficient number of repetitions.

- Drill should be conducted from both a left and right handoff alignment.

Coaching Points:

- Always check to see that all personnel are aligned correctly and are in their proper stances.

- Instruct the running backs to focus their eyes straight ahead when receiving the handoff.

- Emphasize the importance of securing the football through the collision and gauntlet areas.
- Instruct the running backs to keep their shoulders *squared* and to run on the *rise* as they run through the gauntlet.

Safety Considerations:

- Proper warm-up should precede drill.
- Instruct the defenders in the collision area not to be abusive as they *jam* the running backs.
- Instruct the running backs always to run with their heads up.

Variations:

- Can remove quarterback and use as a tight end and wide receiver drill.
- Can remove quarterback and use as a defensive back and linebacker drill. (Coach can throw an interception and have defenders run the gauntlet.)

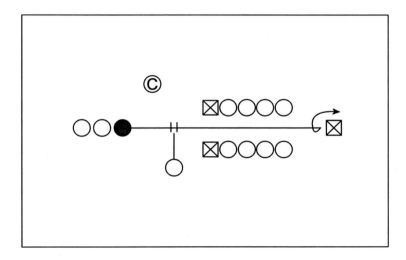

FULLBACK-SWEEP BLOCK*

Terry M. Donahue

University of Kansas, University of California at Los Angeles, San Francisco 49ers
College Football Hall of Fame: 2000

Objective: To teach and practice the proper fundamentals and techniques in the execution of the fullback's block on the sweep play. This block may vary according to the play of the defense, and the fullback must be able to adjust his block as the play develops.

Equipment Needed: Three cones, one hand shield, and footballs

Description:

- Align a center, quarterback, fullback, and running back over the football on a selected line of scrimmage.

- Position three cones three-yards apart and perpendicular to the line of scrimmage across from the offensive tackle position. These cones define the inside boundary of the sweep.

- A defender holding a hand shield is aligned anywhere between the inside linebacker and outside rolled-up cornerback positions. He is instructed to stop the sweep play from any position, from any angle, and with varying degrees of penetration across the line of scrimmage.

- On quarterback cadence and ball snap, the offense executes the toss sweep with the fullback adjusting his block according to the way the defender plays.

- The drill continues until all drill participants have had a sufficient number of repetitions.

- The drill should be conducted both left and right and from various field positions.

Coaching Points:

- Always check to see that all personnel are aligned correctly and are in their proper stances.

- Instruct the fullbacks to take an angle toward the defender that will make it impossible for the defender to move under their blocks without allowing the ballcarriers to go to the outside, or move around the fullbacks without giving the ballcarrier a lane to the inside.

*Reprinted with permission from 101 Winning Football Drills: From the Legends of the Game by Jerry Tolley

- Instruct the ballcarrier always to stay behind and stay deeper than the fullback.

- To block an inside linebacker penetrating to the inside, the fullbacks should execute a shoulder block. To block a cornerback penetrating to the outside, the fullbacks should use a reverse-body block. A rolling-body block should be used against an outside penetrator who plays with a low, hard shoulder pad.

Safety Considerations:

- Proper warm-up should precede the drill.

- The drill area should be clear of all foreign articles.

- The drill should progress from walk-through to full speed.

- The coach should monitor closely the intensity of the drill.

- Instruct all fullbacks as to the proper fundamentals and techniques of the various blocks to be executed.

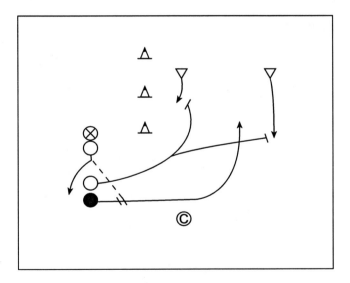

HIT AND SPLIT TO SIDELINE

Thomas K. Moore
Wichita State University, Clemson University, The Citadel

Objective: To teach and practice the proper fundamentals and techniques of running the football.

Equipment Needed: Four long shields and footballs

Description:

- Position two defenders with long shields one yard apart on the right hash mark of a selected line of scrimmage. Additional shield holders are positioned 10 and 20 yards downfield and four yards from the near sideline (see diagram).

- Align a row of running backs, with football in hand, five yards in front of the first two shield holders.

- The coach is positioned downfield adjacent to the shield holders in that area.

- On coach's command, the first running back secures the football and drives through the first two shield holders as they impede his run by *jamming* him with their shields. He then cuts and sprints toward the near sideline.

- When he reaches the sideline area, he cuts upfield, lowers his shoulders, and strives to stay in bounds as the two shield holders, in turn, try to force him out of bounds.

- Drill continues until all running backs have had a sufficient number of repetitions.

- Drill should be conducted from both the left and right hash marks.

Coaching Points:

- Instruct the running backs to keep their head up at all times.

- Emphasize the importance of *dipping* and *squaring* the shoulders and securing the football through the first collision area.

- Instruct the running backs to carry the football under the outside arm and to attack the sideline shield holders with a low forearm-shoulder blow.

- Insist that the drill be conducted at full speed.

Safety Considerations:

- Proper warm-up should precede drill.

- Drill area (including sideline areas) should be clear of all foreign articles.

- Instruct the defenders in the collision areas not to be abusive as they *jam* the running backs and never *jam* them in the head area.

Variations:

- Can be used with the order of the shields reversed (sideline shields first and paired shields 10 or 20 yards downfield).

- Can be used as a tight end or wide receiver drill.

- Can be used as a conditioning drill.

- Can be used as a motivational drill by timing individual performances.

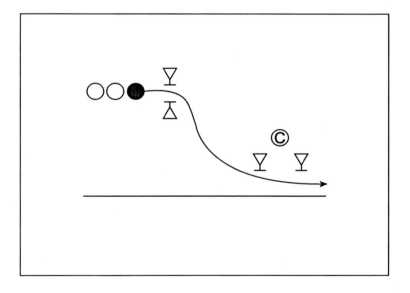

HIGH KNEE–HANG ON–HIT*

Ben Schwartzwalder (Deceased)
Muhlenberg College, Syracuse University
National Champions: Syracuse 1959
National Coach of the Year: Syracuse 1959
College Football Hall of Fame: 1982
Amos Alonzo Stagg Award: 1977
AFCA President: 1967

Objective: To teach and practice the proper fundamentals and techniques of running and securing the football, with a special emphasis on high knee action, leg drive, and power.

Equipment Needed: Three large blocking dummies, two hand shields, and footballs

Description:

- Lay three large blocking dummies one-yard apart and parallel to each other (see diagram).

- Align two rows of linemen just behind dummy area. Two yards separate the two rows of linemen.

- Two additional linemen holding hand shields are positioned behind the two rows of linemen.

- Position a row of running backs five yards in front of the first blocking dummy.

- On the coach's command, the first running back sprints over the dummies and then runs through the gauntlet of linemen as they try to jerk the football from his hands.

- After clearing the gauntlet, the running back lowers his shoulders and explodes through the defenders holding the hand shields as they try to impede his progress.

- The drill continues until all running backs have had a sufficient number of repetitions.

*Reprinted with permission from *101 Winning Football Drills: From the Legends of the Game* by Jerry Tolley

Coaching Points:

- Emphasize the importance of a quick start and high-knee lifts through the dummy area.

- Emphasize the importance of securing the football through the gauntlet and collision areas.

- Instruct the running backs to lower their center of gravity as they explode through the collision area.

Safety Considerations:

- It is imperative that proper warm-up precede the drill.

- Instruct the linemen in the collision area not to be abusive as they *jam* the running backs.

Variation:

- Can be used as a tight end and wide receiver drill.

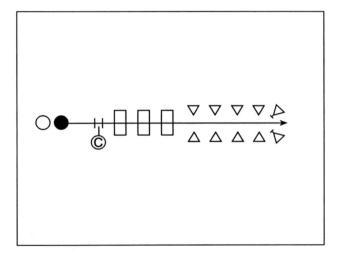

READ AND HANDOFF DRILL

Elmer G. Redd (Deceased)
University of Houston

Objective: To teach and practice the proper fundamentals and techniques of running the football. Incorporated are skills related to quickness, reaction, and agility.

Equipment Needed: Twenty truck tires and footballs

Description:

- Place five stacks of tires four high and three feet apart as shown in diagram. The tires should be positioned between the 10- and five-yard lines.
- Position a quarterback, holding a football, in a dive relationship to a row of running backs in front of the stacks of tires.
- The coach is positioned behind the middle stack of tires.
- On quarterback's cadence and snap count, the first running back drives from his stance and receives the handoff. He then runs between the first two stacks of tires.
- The coach reacts to the handoff and appears from behind the middle stack of tires and the running back cuts in the opposite direction. He now moves up and around the middle tires and between the back two stacks of tires into the end zone for the score.
- Drill continues until all running backs have had a sufficient number of repetitions.
- Drill should be conducted from both left and right handoff alignments.

Coaching Points:

- Always check to see that all personnel are aligned correctly and are in their proper stances.
- Insist that the handoff be executed properly.
- Instruct the running backs to focus on the middle stack of tires as they receive the handoff.
- Insist that the drill be conducted at full speed.

Safety Considerations:

- Proper warm-up should precede drill.
- It is imperative that tires be stacked four high to prevent tripping.
- Helmets should be worn with chinstraps snapped.

Variations:

- Can be used with defenders placed behind the back two stacks of tires to try to jerk the football away from the running back.
- Can be used with dummies or shield holders positioned behind the tire area.

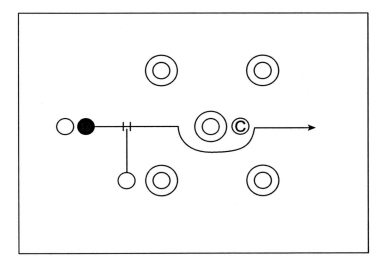

RUNNING-PASS DRILL*

Don B. Faurot (Deceased)
Truman State University, University of Missouri
College Football Hall of Fame: 1961
Amos Alonzo Stagg Award: 1964
AFCA President: 1953

Objective: To teach and practice the proper fundamentals and techniques in the execution of the halfback pass off the option play.

Equipment Needed: Footballs

Description:

- Align an offense (center, quarterback, running back, and wide receiver) over the football on a selected line of scrimmage.

- Position a cornerback in his regular alignment over the wide receiver.

- Other drill participants stand adjacent to their drill area.

- On quarterback's cadence and ball snap, the offense executes the halfback-option pass as the running back keys the cornerback.

- If cornerback attacks line of scrimmage, running back passes the football to wide receiver on a flag pattern. If cornerback covers receiver, running back tucks football away and sprints downfield.

- The drill continues until all drill participants have had a sufficient number of repetitions.

- The drill should be conducted both left and right and from various positions on the field.

Coaching Points:

- Always check to see that all personnel are aligned correctly and are in their proper stances.

- Instruct the running backs to key the cornerback and to make the play look like an option run.

- Make sure all running backs practice the proper mechanics in throwing all passes.

---

*Reprinted with permission from *101 Winning Football Drills: From the Legends of the Game* by Jerry Tolley

Safety Considerations:

- Proper warm-up should precede the drill.
- The drill area (including sideline areas) should be clear of all foreign articles.
- This is not recommended as a contact drill.

Variations:

- Can incorporate a tight end.
- Can be used from various formations.
- Can be used as a wide-receiver drill.
- Can be used as a defensive-back drill.

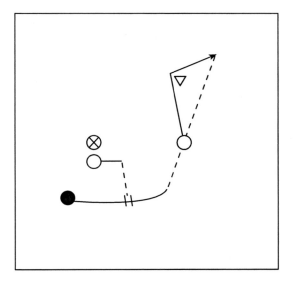

ROCKY ROAD

Vito E. Ragazzo
University of North Carolina, Virginia Military Academy, East Carolina University,
Wake Forest University, New England Patriots, Shippensburg University,
Virginia Polytechnic Institute and State University
National Coach of the Year: Shippensburg 1981

Objective: To teach and practice the proper fundamentals and techniques of running the football. Incorporated are skills related to receiving the handoff, explosion, and open field running.

Equipment Needed: Line-spacing strip, six hand shields, and footballs

Description:

- Place a line-spacing strip on the left hash mark of the plus-40-yard line.

- Position two defenders (side by side) holding shields midway between the hash mark and sideline on the line of scrimmage. A third defender holding a shield is placed five yards behind the paired shield holders. Three additional defenders, also holding hand shields, are placed three yards from the sideline on the plus-30-, plus-25-, and plus-20-yard lines. A row of tacklers is positioned at the hash mark area on the goal line (see diagram).

- Align a row of running backs, center, and quarterback over the football on the line-spacing strip.

- On cadence and ball snap, the quarterback pitches the football to the first running back.

- The running back takes the pitch and *explodes* through the paired shield holders on the sideline, stiff arms the next, and sprints down the sideline by the three remaining defenders as those shield holders try to force him out of bounds.

- After the running back passes the last shield holder, he sprints past the goal line tackler and into the end zone.

- Drill continues until all running backs have had a sufficient number of repetitions.

- Drill should be conducted from both the left and right hash marks.

Coaching Points:

- Always check to see that all personnel are aligned correctly and are in their proper stances.

- Instruct all running backs to carry the football under the outside arm and to secure the football through the collision areas.

- Insist that the drill be conducted at full speed.

Safety Considerations:

- Proper warm-up should precede drill.

- Drill area (including sideline areas) should be clear of all foreign articles.

- Instruct the defenders in the collision areas not to be abusive as they *jam* the running backs.

Variations:

- Can be used with various offensive plays (dive, option, etc.).

- Can be used as an open field tackling drill.

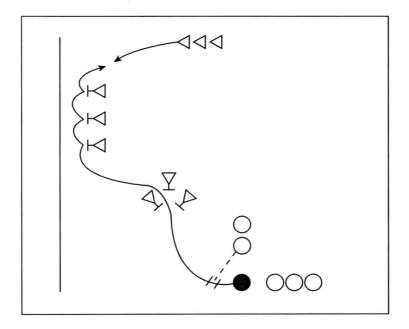

SIDELINE DRILL*

J. Frank Broyles
Baylor University, Georgia Insititute of Technology, University of Missouri,
University of Arkansas
National Champions: Arkansas 1964
National Coach of the Year: Arkansas 1964
College Football Hall of Fame: 1983
AFCA President: 1970

Objective: To teach and practice the proper fundamentals and techniques of running the football with special emphasis on staying in bounds.

Equipment Needed: Three hand shields and footballs

Description:

- Align an offense (center, quarterback, and running back) over the football on the left-hash mark of a selected line of scrimmage.

- Position three defenders, holding hand shields, four-yards apart and three yards from the near sideline. The first shield holder stands on the line of scrimmage.

- Other drill participants stand adjacent to the drill area.

- On quarterback's cadence and ball snap, the first running back drives from his stance, takes the pitch, sprints to the sideline, and cuts upfield. He then runs past the three shield holders as they try to force him out of bounds.

- The drill continues until all running backs have had a sufficient number of repetitions.

- The drill should be conducted from both the left and right hash marks.

Coaching Points:

- Always check to see that all personnel are aligned correctly and are in their proper stances.

- Insist that all running backs carry the football under the outside arm.

- Instruct the running backs to lower their shoulders and to drive into each shield holder with an inside forearm-shoulder blow.

- Insist that the drill be conducted at full speed.

*Reprinted with permission from 101 Winning Football Drills: From the Legends of the Game by Jerry Tolley

Safety Considerations:

- Proper warm-up should precede the drill.

- The drill area (including sideline areas) should be clear of all foreign articles.

- Instruct shield holders not to abuse the running backs and never *jam* them in the head area.

Variations:

- Can be used with a varying number of shield holders.

- Can be used with different backfield actions.

- Can be used as a center-quarterback ball-exchange drill.

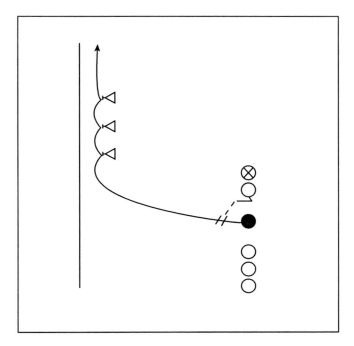

THE ISOLATION PLAY

Art Baker

Clemson University, Texas Tech University, Florida State University, Furman University, The Citadel, East Carolina University, University of South Carolina

Objective: To teach and practice the proper fundamentals and techniques in the execution of the isolation play.

Equipment Needed: Two blocking dummies, three hand shields, and footballs

Description:

- Position an offense (center, quarterback, fullback, and tailback) over the football on the five-yard line.

- Place a linebacker holding a hand shield in his normal position. Two additional defenders, with hand shields, are positioned side by side behind the linebacker and on the one-yard line.

- At the point of attack, lay two blocking dummies five yards apart and vertical to the line of scrimmage (see diagram).

- Other drill participants stand adjacent to the drill area.

- On quarterback's cadence, the ball is snapped and the offense executes the isolation play.

- The fullback leads the play and drives the linebacker from the path of the play.

- The tailback runs behind the fullback's blocks and then *explodes* through the paired shield holders for the score.

- Drill continues until all personnel have had a sufficient number of repetitions.

- Drill should be conducted both left and right and from various five-yard line alignments.

Coaching Points:

- Always check to see that all personnel are aligned correctly and are in their proper stances.

- Emphasis should be placed on all the fundamentals and techniques that are taught in the execution of the isolation play.

Safety Considerations:

- Proper warm-up should precede drill.

- The drill should progress from walk-through to full speed.

- Instruct all fullbacks as to the proper fundamentals and techniques of the block to be executed on the linebackers.

- The coach should monitor closely the intensity of the drill—particularly during the fullback's block on the linebacker.

- Instruct the paired defenders not be abusive as they *jam* the running backs and to never jam them in the head area.

Variations:

- Can be used with other lead blocking plays.

- Can be used with the quarterback passing to a wide receiver after executing the isolation handoff. (Position another player to toss the quarterback a second football.)

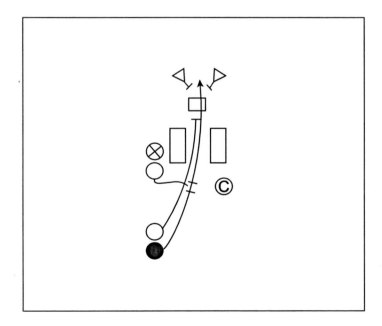

THREE-IN-ONE

Emory D. Bellard
University of Texas, Texas A&M University, Mississippi State University
National Coach of the Year: Texas A&M 1975

Objective: To teach and practice the proper fundamentals of receiving a handoff, exploding through the line, and running with the football.

Equipment Needed: Four large blocking dummies, two hand shields, and footballs

Description:

- Align two defenders, holding hand shields (side by side) on a selected line of scrimmage.

- Lay three blocking dummies one behind the other and one yard behind the two defenders with hand shields. The blocking dummies are placed parallel to the line of scrimmage and two yards separate each dummy. A defender holds a fourth blocking dummy eight yards downfield (see diagram).

- The quarterback (coach) stands to either side of the front of the drill area and in a dive relationship to a row of running backs.

- On coach's cadence and snap count, the first running back drives from his stance and receives handoff from coach. He then blasts through the paired hand shields, high steps over and through the three dummies, and sprints to the final defender. Now he drives into the dummy with a forearm-shoulder blow and then spins either left or right and sprints 10 yards upfield.

- Drill continues until all running backs have had a sufficient number of repetitions.

- Drill should be conducted from both left and right handoff alignments.

Coaching Points:

- Always check to see that running backs are aligned correctly and are in their proper stances.

- Instruct the running backs to focus their eyes straight ahead when receiving the handoff.

- Emphasize the importance of driving the legs and securing the football through the collision areas.

- Insist that the drill be conducted at full speed.

Safety Considerations:

- Proper warm-up should precede drill.

- Instruct the shield holders not to abuse the running backs and never *jam* them in the head area.

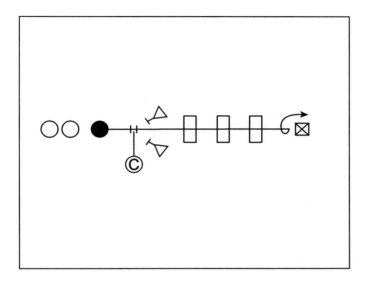

TIRE DRILL*

Dr. James "Jim" Wacker (Deceased)
Concordia College (Nebraska), Augustana College (South Dakota),
Texas Lutheran University, North Dakota State University,
Southwest Texas State University, Texas Christian University, University of Minnesota
National Champions: Texas Lutheran 1974 and 1975;
Southwest Texas State 1981 and 1982
National Coach of the Year: Southwest Texas 1982; Texas Christian 1984

Objective: To teach and practice the proper fundamentals and techniques of running the football. Incorporated are skills related to reading, reacting, and acceleration.

Equipment Needed: 20 car tires, three blocking dummies, and footballs

Description:

- Position five stacks of tires (four high) as shown in the diagram. The distance between the stacks of tires varies according to the skill level of the running backs.

- Place three blocking dummies in a row and parallel to the back two stacks of tires. Two yards separate each of the three dummies.

- Position a quarterback, holding a football, in a dive relationship to a row of running backs in front of the tires.

- The coach or manager stands behind the middle stack of tires.

- On quarterback's cadence and snap count, the first running back drives from his stance and receives the handoff. He runs between the first two stacks of tires as the coach appears from behind either side of the middle tires.

- The running back now cuts in the opposite direction. He then moves up and around the middle tires and between the back two stacks of tires.

- Now the running back accelerates over and through the three blocking dummies.

- The drill continues until all running backs have had a sufficient number of repetitions.

- The drill should be conducted from both left- and right-handoff alignments.

*Reprinted with permission from *101 Winning Football Drills: From the Legends of the Game* by Jerry Tolley

Coaching Points:

- Always check to see that the running backs are aligned correctly and are in their proper stances.
- Instruct the running backs to make as sharp a cut as possible.
- Make sure the running backs accelerate over and through the dummy area.
- Make sure that all quarterbacks carry out all fakes after executing the handoff.
- Insist that the drill be conducted at full speed.

Safety Consideration:

- Proper warm-up should precede the drill.

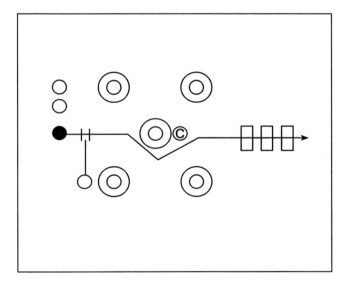

WET-BALL DRILL*

Fred S. Akers
University of Wyoming, University of Texas, Purdue University
National Coach of the Year: Texas 1977

Objective: To teach and practice the proper fundamentals and techniques of receiving and running with a wet football. Incorporated are skills related to reaction, agility, and quickness.

Equipment Needed: Eight large blocking dummies, one bucket of water, and footballs

Description:

• Align two defenders holding blocking dummies one-yard apart on a selected line of scrimmage.

• Lay three blocking dummies one behind the other and one-yard behind the two defenders holding the front dummies. The blocking dummies are placed horizontal to the line of scrimmage and two yards separate each dummy. Alternating running backs are positioned on both sides of each of the three dummies, forming a gauntlet.

• Three additional dummies are held in a triangular relationship seven-yards behind the front three dummies. The coach holds the dummy forming the apex of the triangle (see diagram).

• The quarterback stands to either side of the front of the drill area and in a selected play relationship to a running back. He holds a wet football taken from a water bucket adjacent to his drill area.

• On cadence and snap count, the running back drives from his stance and receives the wet football from the quarterback. He then blasts through the paired dummies and sprints over and through the three dummies as the alternating running back tries to jerk the football from his hands.

• After clearing the gauntlet area, the running back sprints toward the triangle-dummy area as the coach tilts his dummy either left or right. The running back breaks in the opposite direction and runs through the back two held dummies.

• The drill continues until all running backs have had a sufficient number of repetitions.

• The drill should be conducted from both a left- and right-handoff alignment.

*Reprinted with permission from *101 Winning Football Drills: From the Legends of the Game* by Jerry Tolley

Coaching Points:

- Always check to see that running backs are aligned correctly and are in their proper stances.

- Emphasize the importance of body lean, good leg action, and securing the football throughout the drill.

- Insist that the drill be conducted at full speed.

Safety Considerations:

- Proper warm-up should precede the drill.

- Instruct the defenders in the collision area not to be abusive as they jam the running back.

Variation:

- Can be used with a dry football.

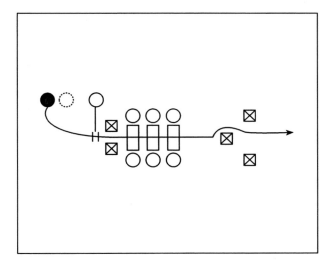

RAG DRILL

Otis J. Washington
Southern University, Louisiana State University

Objective: To develop general agility, footwork, quickness, balance, and body control.

Equipment Needed: Four rags and footballs

Description:

- Place four rags 10 yards apart forming a square (see diagram).

- Align a row of running backs in a straight line 10 yards from and facing one of the rags.

- On coach's command, the first running back, with football in hand, sprints to and executes a 360-degree revolution around the first rag. He then sprints to the second rag and again executes the 360-degree revolution. The procedure is repeated for the third and fourth rags.

- Drill continues until all running backs have had a sufficient number of repetitions.

- Drill should be conducted in both clockwise and counter-clockwise directions.

Coaching Points:

- Instruct the running backs to place their inside hands on the rags as they execute each 360-degree revolution.

- Make sure that running backs maintain a fundamentally sound body position throughout the drill.

- Insist that the drill be conducted at full speed.

Safety Considerations:

- Proper warm-up should precede drill.

- Maintain a minimum distance of 10 yards between performing drill participants.

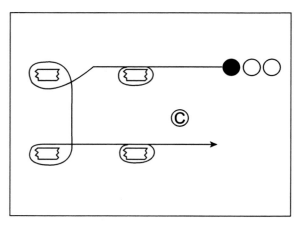

Variation:

- Can be used as a general agility drill.

2

Offensive Line Drills

QUICK SET WITH PUNCH

George O'Leary
Syracuse University, San Diego Chargers, Georgia Institute of Technology,
Minnesota Vikings, University of Central Florida
National Coach of the Year: Georgia Tech 2000

Objective: To teach and practice the proper fundamentals and techniques in executing the quick punch from the pass set position.

Equipment Needed: Punch balls

Description:

- Align a row of five linemen three yards apart on a selected line of scrimmage. Each lineman is positioned in a two- or a three-point stance depending on the scheme used.

- Position a defender, with a *punch ball* in hand, two to three yards in front of each offensive lineman.

- The coach is positioned behind the offensive linemen (see diagram).

- On coach's cadence and snap count, the offensive linemen move to their designated *pass set* positions.

- The defenders react to the movement of the offensive linemen and deliver the *punch ball* with a *sharp* pass to the chest of the front-facing offensive lineman.

- The offensive lineman *punches* the delivered *punch ball* while remaining in proper *pass set* position. (If the offensive linemen execute the *punch* technique correctly, the *punch balls* should return to the defenders).

- The offensive linemen now return to their *pass set* positions and, on coach's command, descriptions five and six are repeated.

- The offensive linemen again return to their *pass set* positions and, on coach's command, descriptions five and six are repeated once more.

- Drill continues until all offensive linemen have had a sufficient number of repetitions in executing the *quick punch* technique.

Coaching Points:

- Always check to see that offensive linemen are aligned correctly and are in their proper stances.

- In moving to the pass set position, the offensive linemen should have their head, shoulders and chest behind their knees.

- Instruct the offensive linemen to always have their elbows in and the thumbs forming a (W) when contacting the punch ball while executing the quick punch technique.

Safety Considerations:

- Proper warm-up should precede drill.

- Drill area should be clear of all foreign articles.

- Helmets should be worn with chinstraps strapped.

Variations:

- Can be used with a basketball or medicine ball.

- Drill can be initiated either by the coach's cadence and snap count or by the movement of the offensive linemen.

- Can be used with the defenders aligned on inside or outside *shade* position.

- Can be used without a *punch ball*. If a *punch ball* is not used, the defenders must be positioned close enough to the offensive linemen to be able to reach out and grab the shoulders of the offensive linemen. When the drill is conducted in this manner, the defender is instructed to give up his chest to the offensive lineman as he grabs the shoulders and attempts to pull the offensive lineman forward.

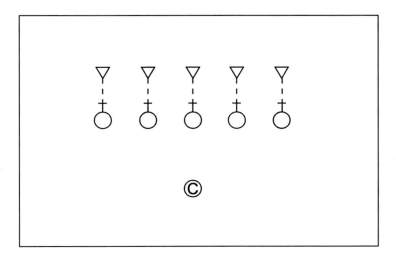

EXPLOSION PROGRESSION DRILL

Michael C. Barry
University of Arizona, San Antonio Gunslingers, New Orleans/Portland Breakers,
Southern Illinois University, Iowa State University, University of Colorado,
University of Southern California, University of Tennessee,
North Carolina State University

Objective: To teach and practice the proper fundamentals and techniques in the execution of the shoulder-forearm block. Special emphasis is placed on hip extension.

Equipment Needed: Seven-man sled

Description:

- Align offensive personnel (center, two guards and two tackles) in a *shade* relationship to the pads of the seven-man sled. Assign four sled riders. All other personnel fall in behind the front line. The drill is conducted in three phases as follows:
  - o Forearm blow. Linemen are aligned in the *football position* in a *shade* relationship to the pads of the seven-man sled. On coach's command, linemen deliver four right forearm blows to the sled in succession. Repeat with the left shoulders.
  - o Shoulder-forearm blow. Linemen are again aligned in the *football position*. On coach's command, all linemen deliver four right forearm-shoulder blocks to the sled in succession. Repeat with left forearm-shoulder blocks.
  - o Six-point explosion drill. Linemen are positioned in six-point stances and three feet in front of the pads of the sled. On coach's command, all linemen fire out and execute four right forearm-shoulder blocks to the sled in succession (the hips, knees, and ankles are fully extended). Again the description is repeated with left forearm-shoulder blocks.
- Drill continues until all linemen have had a sufficient number of repetitions in executing the three phases of the drill.

Coaching Points:

- In contacting the pad, make sure the arm is bent to form a 90-degree blocking surface angle with the wrist rotated inward.

- Instruct linemen to *shoot* the opposite arm and hand up and beyond the pad.

- In executing the forearm-shoulder block from the six-point stance, insist that all linemen fully extend their hips, knees, and ankles.
- Make sure all linemen use the proper fundamentals and techniques in the execution of all forearm-shoulder blocks.

Safety Considerations:

- Proper warm-up should precede drill.
- Helmets should be worn with chinstraps snapped.
- Drill should progress from half speed to full speed.
- Instruct sled riders to hold firmly to the sled.
- The sled should be checked periodically for possible maintenance and repairs.

Variations:

- Can position linemen six inches away from the pad of the sled in a six-point stance and practice forearm blows.
- Can be used for all offensive positions.

BOARD-DRIVE DRILL*

Phillip Fulmer
Wichita State University, Vanderbilt University, University of Tennessee
National Champions: Tennessee 1998
National Coach of the Year: Tennessee 1998
AFCA President: 2003

Objective: To teach and practice the proper fundamentals and techniques in the execution of the drive block.

Equipment Needed: Five boards (6" x 2" x 8') and five large blocking dummies

Description:

- Place five boards (6" x 2" x 8') perpendicular to a selected line of scrimmage. Approximately five feet separate each board.

- Align an offensive line in three-point stances straddling the midpoint of the boards.

- Position defenders holding dummies in a straddling position across from the offensive line.

- Alternating offensive lines stand behind the performing drill participants.

- On coach's cadence and snap count, the offensive linemen explode out of their stances and execute drive blocks on the defenders, driving them off the end of the boards.

- The defenders react to the movement of the offensive linemen and take a step forward to resist their blocks.

- The drill continues until all offensive lines have had a sufficient number of repetitions.

Coaching Points:

- Always check to see that the linemen are in their proper stances.

- Instruct the linemen to contact the dummy with heads up, shoulders squared to the defender, and feet shoulder-width apart.

- Make sure the linemen use the proper fundamentals and techniques in the execution of the drive block.

---

*Reprinted with permission from *101 Winning Football Drills: From the Legends of the Game* by Jerry Tolley

Safety Considerations:

- Proper warm-up should precede the drill.
- The drill should progress from walk-through, to half speed, to full speed.
- The coach should monitor closely the intensity of the drill.
- The boards should be beveled and checked for splinters daily.
- Instruct the linemen as to the proper fundamentals and techniques of the drive block.

Variation:

- Can incorporate tight ends.

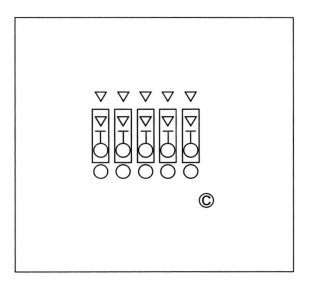

HIT AND STICK

J. Rex Dockery (Deceased)
University of Tennessee, Georgia Institute of Technology, Vanderbilt University,
Texas Tech University, Memphis State University

Objective: To teach and practice the proper fundamentals and techniques of driving off the line of scrimmage and sustaining a shoulder block.

Equipment Needed: Four hand shields

Description:

- Align four offensive linemen in their stances on a selected line of scrimmage. Five yards separate each of the four linemen.

- Position a shield holder head-up to each lineman. Six inches separate the linemen and shield holders.

- Other drill participants stand adjacent to drill area.

- The drill is conducted in two phases as follows:
    - Explosion off the line. On coach's command, all linemen *roll out* and *explode* from their stances (do not step) into a *layout* position on the shield. After contact, blockers return to the start position and the *layout* technique is repeated three more times.
    - Sustaining the block. This phase of the drill begins with the linemen in the *layout* position on the shields. On coach's command, the blockers drive their feet as the shield holders retreat slowly, changing their direction as they retreat. The blockers maintain contact with the shield until the whistle blows. The description is repeated two more times.

- Drill continues until all personnel have had a sufficient number of repetitions in executing both phases.

Coaching Points:

- Always check to see that linemen are in their proper stances (phase one only).

- Instruct linemen to contact the hand shield on the rise with their shoulders *square* to the shield, head up and feet shoulder-width apart.

- In the sustaining the block phase of the drill it is important that the linemen achieve a good *layout* position before the command is given for the defenders to retreat.

Safety Considerations:

- Proper warm-up should precede drill.

- Drill area should be clear of all foreign articles.

- Helmets should be worn with chinstraps snapped.

- In sustaining the block the linemen must maintain pressure on the shield at all times.

- Maintain a minimum distance of five yards between each pair of paired drill participants.

INDIVIDUAL PASS PROTECTION

Tom D. Reed
Miami University (Ohio), University of Akron, University of Arizona,
University of Michigan, North Carolina State University

Objective: To teach and practice the proper fundamentals and techniques of executing the pass block.

Equipment Needed: Four cones and one large blocking dummy

Description:

- Place two cones three yards apart on a selected line of scrimmage. A second pair of cones is placed six yards apart and five yards behind the first pair. A standup dummy (quarterback) is positioned five yards behind and centered between the second set of cones (see diagram).

- Position an offensive lineman in his stance on the line of scrimmage midway between the first two cones. Position a second offensive lineman in a *pass set* position between the second set of cones.

- A pass rusher is placed over the first lineman and is instructed to use a variety of pass rushing techniques in rushing the passer.

- Other drill participants stand adjacent to drill area.

- On coach's cadence and snap count, the first offensive lineman executes his pass block on the charging defender.

- If and when the defender defeats the pass block of the first offensive lineman, the second lineman executes his pass block.

- The drill ends on a whistle either when the pass rusher is totally stopped by the pass protectors or when the defender tags the (quarterback) dummy.

- Drill continues until all drill participants have had a sufficient number of repetitions.

Coaching Points:

- Always check to see that first linemen are in their proper stance and that the second linemen are in their correct *pass set* positions.

- Insist that all linemen maintain the proper body alignment throughout the drill.

- Make sure all linemen use the proper fundamentals and techniques of pass protection.

- The second linemen are instructed never to cross the line between the second set of cones.

Safety Considerations:

- It is imperative that proper warm-up precede drill.
- The coach should watch for and eliminate all unacceptable match-ups as to size and athletic ability.
- Instruct all linemen as to the proper fundamentals and techniques of pass blocking.
- Instruct the linemen never to *cut block* the pass rushers.
- Never allow both offensive linemen to block the pass rusher at the same time.
- The coach should monitor closely the intensity of the drill.
- A quick whistle is imperative with this drill.

Variations:

- The second set of cones can be placed at various positions to simulate different quarterback pass drops.
- Can be used as a defensive line drill.

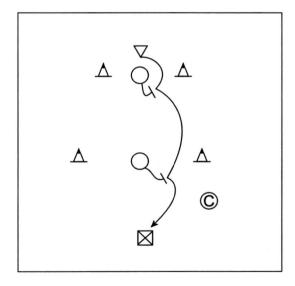

BODY BALANCE–EQUILIBRIUM–HITTING DRILL*

Charles B. "Bud" Wilkinson (Deceased)
Syracuse University, University of Minnesota, University of Oklahoma,
St. Louis Cardinals
National Champions: Oklahoma 1950, 1955, and 1956
National Coach of the Year: Oklahoma 1949
College Football Hall of Fame: 1969
Amos Alonzo Stagg Award: 1984
AFCA President: 1958

Objective: To teach and practice the proper techniques of getting off the ground, regaining balance, and executing a shoulder-drive block.

Equipment Needed: Two-man sled

Description:

- Align two rows of linemen five yards in front of the pads of a two-man sled.

- On the coach's command, the first two drill participants explode from their stances, execute a forward roll, regain their balance, and execute shoulder-drive blocks on the sled.

- After driving the sled for three yards, the linemen disengage the sled and return to the ends of the opposite lines.

- The drill continues until all linemen have executed a sufficient number of forward rolls and left and right shoulder blocks.

Coaching Points:

- Always check to see that the linemen are in their proper stances.

- Insist that the forward roll be performed correctly.

- Instruct linemen to lower their center of gravity, keeping their feet shoulder-width apart as they contact the sled.

- Make sure the linemen use the proper fundamentals and techniques in the execution of all shoulder blocks.

*Reprinted with permission from *101 Winning Football Drills: From the Legends of the Game* by Jerry Tolley

Safety Considerations:

- Proper warm-up should precede the drill.

- The drill area should be clear of all foreign articles.

- Helmets should be worn with chinstraps snapped.

- Instruct the linemen as to the proper fundamentals and techniques of executing the shoulder block and hitting the sled.

- The sled should be checked periodically for possible maintenance and repairs.

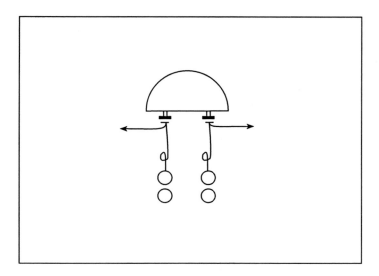

LOVERSLANE

David Kent Moore
University of Louisville, University of Evansville

Objective: To teach and practice the proper fundamentals and techniques in executing the pass block.

Equipment Needed: One large blocking dummy

Description:

- Align an offensive line (center, two guards, and two tackles) in their normal positions on a selected line of scrimmage.

- Position defensive linemen *nose-on-nose* to each offensive player.

- A dummy (quarterback) is placed at various quarterback pass drop positions behind the offense.

- Other drill personnel stand adjacent to drill area.

- The coach stands behind the defense and in turn signals each offensive lineman as to his pass protection assignment and the snap count.

- On coach's cadence and snap count, the designated lineman executes his pass block assignment on the charging pass rusher.

- Drill ends on a whistle either when the pass rusher is blocked or when he tags the (quarterback) dummy.

- Drill continues until all drill participants have had a sufficient number of repetitions.

Coaching Points:

- Always check to see that linemen are aligned correctly and are in their proper stances.

- Insist that all blockers maintain the proper pass blocking alignment throughout the drill.

- Instruct the linemen to *slide* their feet (in the manner of a boxer) and not *chop* their feet.

- Make sure all linemen use the proper fundamentals and techniques of pass blocking.

Safety Considerations:

- It is imperative that proper warm-up precede drill.
- Drill area should be clear of all foreign articles.
- The coach should watch for and eliminate all unacceptable match-ups as to size and athletic abilities.
- The coach should monitor closely the intensity of the drill.
- Instruct the pass blockers never to *cut block* the pass rushers.
- Instruct all offensive linemen as to the proper fundamentals and techniques of pass blocking.
- A quick whistle is imperative with this drill.

Variations:

- Can be used with varying degrees of intensity.
- Can be used as a defensive line drill.

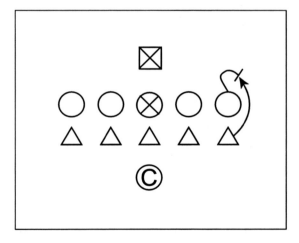

OFFENSIVE LINE BLOCKING DRILL

Rudy Hubbard
Florida A&M University, Ohio State University
National Champions: Florida A&M 1978
National Black College Champions: Florida A&M 1977 and 1978
National Black College Coach of the Year: Florida A&M 1978

Objective: To teach and practice the proper fundamentals and techniques in the execution of various blocking schemes.

Equipment Needed: Footballs

Description:

- Align an offense (center, guards, tackles, tight end, quarterback, and running backs) over the football on a selected line of scrimmage (see diagram).

- Position a scout team defense (nose guard, tackles, ends, and linebackers) over the offense.

- Other drill participants stand adjacent to the drill area.

- The coach stands behind the offense.

- On quarterback's signal, the offense breaks the huddle and executes five plays in rapid succession. Emphasis is placed on executing the different blocking schemes properly.

- The defense reacts to and defeats the blocks of the offensive personnel and pursues the ballcarrier.

- The defense is instructed to change its alignment half way through the drill period.

- Drill continues until all drill participants have had a sufficient number of repetitions.

Coaching Points:

- Always check to see that all offensive linemen are aligned correctly and are in their proper stances.

- Make sure all play assignments are carried out correctly.

- The coach should monitor closely the first three steps of each lineman, watching for over-striding and high blocking.

- Make sure that plays selected attack both sides of the defense.

- The coach should script all plays to be run.

Safety Considerations:

- It is imperative that proper warm-up precede drill.
- Drill area should be clear of all foreign articles.
- The coach should monitor closely the intensity of the drill.
- Instruct offensive linemen to execute all blocks above the waist.
- Under no circumstances are the running backs to be tackled.
- A quick whistle is imperative with this drill.

Variations:

- Can be used as form or live blocking drill.
- Can be used against a variety of defensive alignments.
- Can be used as a defensive line and linebacker drill.

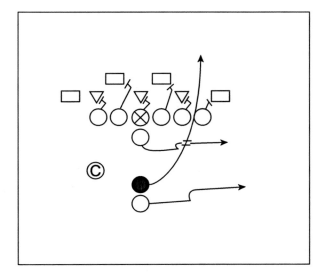

BREAKDOWN OF THE SHOULDER BLOCK*

Harold R. "Tubby" Raymond
University of Maine, University of Delaware
National Champions: Delaware 1971, 1972, and 1979
National Coach of the Year: Delaware 1971, 1972, and 1979
College Football Hall of Fame: 2003
AFCA President: 1981

Objective: To teach and practice the proper fundamentals and techniques in the execution of the shoulder block. Special emphasis is placed on identifying the proper blocking surface.

Equipment Needed: Large blocking dummies

Description:

- Align all the linemen on their hands and knees in front of a firmly held, large blocking dummy. The drill is conducted in four phases as follows:
  - *Phase one*. On the coach's command, have the linemen demonstrate the blocking surface as the front of the shoulder from the neck to the elbow and with the fist in contact with the chest having the shoulders parallel to the ground. The blocking surface should be demonstrated for both the left- and right-shoulder blocks.
  - *Phase two*. On the coach's command, all the linemen explode from the waist driving the right shoulder and forearm into the dummy using the blocking surface as described in phase one. The technique is repeated with the left shoulder.
  - *Phase three*. The linemen stand in a football position one-step away from the held dummy. On the coach's command, all the linemen step with their left foot and drive their right shoulders and forearms into the dummy using the proper blocking surface. The technique is repeated stepping with the right foot and blocking with left shoulder.
  - *Phase four*. The linemen are positioned a short distance from the front of the held dummy. On the coach's command, all the linemen run to and execute a right-shoulder block on the dummy. The technique is repeated using a left-shoulder block.
- The drill continues until all the linemen have had a sufficient number of repetitions in executing the four phases.

*Reprinted with permission from 101 Winning Football Drills: From the Legends of the Game by Jerry Tolley

Coaching Points:

- Always check to see that the linemen are in the desired stance for the execution of each of the four phases.

- Instruct the linemen to keep their shoulders square to the dummy throughout all phases of the drill.

- Insist that the linemen maintain good hitting positions with the head up and feet shoulder-width apart.

- Check for the proper *blocking surface* on the dummies after each block.

Safety Considerations:

- Proper warm-up should precede the drill.

- The drill area should be clear of all foreign articles.

- Helmets should be worn with chinstraps snapped.

- Instruct the dummy holders to maintain a firm grip on the dummies.

Variation:

- Can be used for all positions.

ONE-ON-ONE DRIVE BLOCK

William J. Russo
Lafayette College, Wagner College, Brown University
National Coach of the Year: Lafayette 1988

Objective: To teach and practice the proper fundamentals and techniques in the execution of the drive block.

Equipment Needed: None

Description:

- Align four rows of offensive linemen 10 yards apart and perpendicular to a selected line of scrimmage (see diagram).

- Position a defensive lineman in front of each of the front four offensive linemen.

- The coach stands behind the defenders and signals offensive linemen as to snap count and the block to be executed (reach left, reach right, or straight ahead).

- Now on coach's cadence and snap count, the offensive linemen drive out of their stances and execute the designated block. The defenders react to and defeat the blockers.

- Drill continues until all linemen have executed a sufficient number of repetitions.

Coaching Points:

- Always check to see that all offensive linemen are in their proper stances.

- Insist that all linemen drive out of their stances low and hard focusing on the proper aiming point.

- Instruct linemen to follow through after the initial contact emphasizing proper leg drive.

- Make sure the linemen use the proper fundamentals and techniques in the execution of all drive blocks.

Safety Considerations:

- Drill area should be clear of all foreign articles.

- The coach should watch for and eliminate all unacceptable match-ups as to size and athletic ability.

- A minimum distance of 10 yards should separate each pair of paired drill participants.
- Instruct all linemen as to the proper fundamentals and techniques of the drive block.
- The drill should progress from form to live blocking.
- The coach should monitor closely the intensity of drill.
- A quick whistle is imperative with this drill.

Variations:

- Can be used with defensive personnel aligned in various positions (head up and left or right of the offensive lineman).
- Can be used as a pass protection drill. (When used as a pass protection drill, only three lines of offensive linemen should be used.)
- Can be used as a defensive line drill.

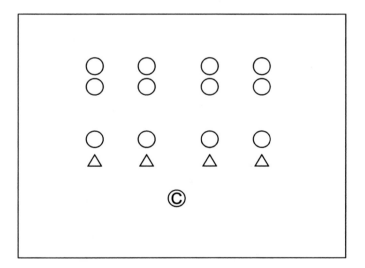

ONE-ON-ONE PASS BLOCKING DRILL

Mark A. Weber
Eastern New Mexico University, West Texas State University, Oregon State University,
Missouri Western State University, University of Nevada,
University of Nevada-Las Vegas, University of California at Los Angeles,
Fresno State University

Objective: To teach and practice the proper fundamentals and techniques of executing the pass block. Incorporated are skills related to setting up, hand coordination, and body position.

Equipment Needed: One large blocking dummy

Description:

- Align offensive personnel (center, two guards, and two tackles) in their stances on a selected line of scrimmage.

- Position a defensive lineman *nose-on-nose* over each offensive lineman.

- Other drill participants stand adjacent to drill area.

- Stand a large blocking dummy in a seven-yard pass drop position behind the offensive line.

- The coach also stands behind the offense and signals one or more of the defensive linemen to rush the passer (dummy). A manager is positioned behind the defense and signals offense as to snap count.

- On coach's cadence and snap count, the designated defender(s) rush the passer (dummy) as their front facing offensive lineman (linemen) execute their pass block(s).

- The drill ends either when the offensive lineman has totally stopped the pass rusher or when the pass rusher tags the dummy.

- Drill continues until all offensive linemen have had a sufficient number of repetitions.

Coaching Points:

- Always check to see that all offensive linemen are aligned correctly and are in their proper stances.

- Instruct all linemen to execute their pass *drop setups* correctly and to maintain the proper body positions throughout the drill.

- Make sure all linemen practice the proper fundamentals and techniques in the execution of all pass blocks.

Safety Considerations:

- It is imperative that proper warm-up precede drill.
- Drill area should be clear of all foreign articles.
- The coach should watch for and eliminate all unacceptable match-ups as to size and athletic ability.
- The coach should monitor closely the intensity of the drill.
- When selecting two defenders to rush, make sure there is a defender positioned between them.
- Instruct offensive linemen never to *cut block* the pass rushers.

Variations:

- Can be used with quarterback simulating various pass drop actions.
- Can be used as a defensive line drill.

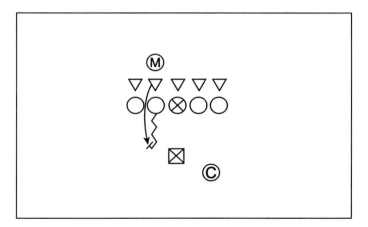

CHUTE DRILL*

Alonzo S. "Jake" Gaither (Deceased)
Florida A&M University
National College Black Champions: 1950, 1952, 1954, 1957, 1959, and 1961
National Coach of the Year: 1961 and 1969
College Football Hall of Fame: 1975
Amos Alonzo Stagg Award: 1974

Objective: To teach and practice the proper fundamentals and techniques of driving out of the stance. Special emphasis is placed on cadence recognition, stance, and maintaining the proper body position.

Equipment Needed: Blocking chute (seven stalls - 36" high x 48" wide), seven boards (14" x 2" x 6'), and footballs

Description:

• Place a board in each of the starting stalls of the blocking chute.

• Align the offensive linemen in waves behind the stalls of the blocking chute.

• The coach stands at either end of the chute.

• On the coach's command, the first wave of linemen take their stances under the chute with the center over the football in the middle stall. A quarterback is positioned over the center.

• On the quarterback's cadence and ball snap, all the linemen drive out of their stances.

• The drill continues until all the linemen have had a sufficient number of repetitions.

Coaching Points:

• Make sure all the linemen are aligned correctly and are in their proper stances.

• Insist that the linemen maintain good body alignment throughout the drill.

• Insist that the drill be conducted at full speed.

---

*Reprinted with permission from *101 Winning Football Drills: From the Legends of the Game* by Jerry Tolley

Safety Considerations:

- Proper warm-up should precede the drill.

- The drill area should be clear of all foreign articles.

- It is imperative that helmets be worn with chinstraps snapped.

- The boards should be beveled and checked for splinters daily.

Variations:

- Can be used with the linemen driving out of their stances at varying distances behind the blocking chute.

- Can be used with the linemen driving out of their stances and blocking dummies.

- Can be used as a tight-end drill.

PASS BLOCKING DRILL

Tony J. Colobro
Bluefield State College, Concord College

Objective: To teach and practice the proper fundamentals and techniques in executing the pass block. Incorporated are skills related to proper weight distribution and footwork.

Equipment Needed: Football

Description:

- Position two offensive linemen in their stances five yards apart on a selected line of scrimmage.
- Align a defensive lineman *nose-on-nose* over each offensive lineman.
- A quarterback, holding a football, is positioned between the two offensive linemen.
- Other drill participants stand adjacent to their drill area (see diagram).
- On cadence and snap count, the quarterback initiates the designated pass drop. The offensive linemen execute their pass protection block against the on rushing defenders.
- Drill continues until all drill offensive lines have had a sufficient number of repetitions.

Coaching Points:

- Always check to see that all offensive linemen are in their proper stances.
- Make sure the linemen maintain good body balance throughout the execution of the pass block.
- Instruct the offensive linemen to keep their bodies between the pass rusher and the quarterback at all times.
- The offensive linemen should always know the quarterback's pass drop alignment.
- Make sure all linemen practice the proper fundamentals and techniques in the execution of all pass blocks.

Safety Considerations:

- It is imperative that proper warm-up precede drill.
- Drill area should be clear of all foreign articles.
- The drill should progress from half speed to live blocking.
- The coach should monitor closely the intensity of the drill.
- Instruct offensive linemen never to *cut block* the pass rushers.
- Instruct pass rushers never to *tee-off* on the pass blockers.

Variations:

- Can be used as a team pass protection drill.
- Can be used as a defensive line drill.

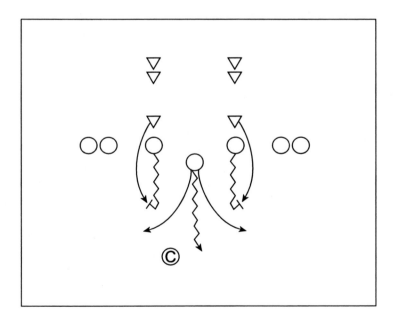

PASS PROGRESSION

William A. "Bill" Curry
Green Bay Packers, Georgia Institute of Technology, University of Alabama,
University of Kentucky
National Coach of the Year: Alabama 1989

Objective: To teach and practice the proper fundamentals and techniques of executing the pass block.

Equipment Needed: None

Description:

- Align all offensive linemen five yards apart on a selected line of scrimmage. Position a pass rusher *nose-on-nose* over each offensive lineman. The drill is conducted in four phases as follows:
  - Set drill. On coach's cadence and snap count, all offensive linemen move from their stances to a *pass set* position.
  - Interval drill. On coach's command, *position*, all linemen move to the *pass set* position. The pass rushers react to movement and approach the offensive linemen. Now the linemen extend their arms contacting the pass rusher in the pectoral area with the heels of their hands. The pass rusher is instructed to stop on contact.
  - One-point mirror drill. On coach's command, *position*, all drill participants react as in the above and with the pass rushers grabbing the shoulder pads of the offensive linemen. On coach's second command, *front*, all personnel move their feet in place. On coach's third command, *move*, pass rushers pull, push, and *jerk* the offensive linemen as offensive linemen try to maintain a *squared* position on the pass rusher. (Blockers are not allowed to use hands and pass rushers are instructed *not* to go at full speed as they execute their pass rushes.)
  - Three-point mirror drill. Same as preceding description except that offensive linemen are now allowed to use hands and pass rushers are instructed to push, pull, and *jerk* at full speed as they execute their pass rushes.
- Drill continues until all offensive linemen have had a sufficient number of repetitions in executing the four phases of the drill.

Coaching Points:

- Always check to see that offensive linemen are in their proper stances.

- Make sure the linemen maintain the proper pass block body position throughout all phases of the drill.

- Instruct the offensive linemen to keep their bodies between the pass rusher and the quarterback at all times.

- Insist that all offensive linemen keep their feet shoulder-width apart and with the outside foot slightly back.

- Make sure all linemen practice the proper fundamentals and techniques in executing the various phases of the drill.

Safety Considerations:

- It is imperative that proper warm-up precede drill.

- Drill area should be clear of all foreign articles.

- A minimum distance of five yards should be maintained between each pair of paired drill participants.

- The coach should monitor closely the intensity of the drill.

- The coach should watch for and eliminate all unacceptable match-ups as to size and athletic ability.

DRIVE-TURN*

Joe V. Paterno
Pennsylvania State University
National Champions: 1982 and 1986
National Coach of the Year: 1968, 1978, 1981, 1982, 1986, 1990, 1994 and 1998
Amos Alonzo Stagg Award: 2002

Objective: To teach and practice the proper fundamentals and techniques of maintaining contact with a defender after the initial block.

Equipment Needed: Two-man sled

Description:

- Position a row of linemen in front of the left pad of a two-man blocking sled.

- The coach stands adjacent to the opposite pad and fixes his hands on the strut.

- On the coach's cadence and snap count, the first lineman drives out of his stance and executes a right-shoulder block to the pad of the sled.

- Just after the lineman begins to drive the sled, the coach turns the sled by pushing and pulling on the strut.

- The drill continues until all the linemen have had a sufficient number of repetitions with both left- and right-shoulder blocks.

Coaching Points:

- Always check to see that linemen are in their proper stances.

- Instruct the linemen to contact the sled with their shoulders square to the pad, heads up, and feet apart.

- It is important that all linemen accelerate their feet and turn their heads into the strut in maintaining control over the sled.

- Make sure the linemen use the proper fundamentals and techniques in the execution of all shoulder blocks.

*Reprinted with permission from 101 Winning Football Drills: From the Legends of the Game by Jerry Tolley

Safety Considerations:

- Proper warm-up should precede the drill.

- The drill area should be clear of all foreign articles.

- Helmets should be worn with chinstraps snapped.

- The coach should not manipulate the sled until the lineman has made contact and has the sled under control.

- The coach should never jerk or move the sled too hard or too rapidly.

- The sled should be checked periodically for possible maintenance and repairs.

Variation:

- Can be used without the coach holding the strut.

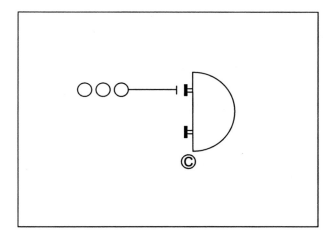

POWER POINT PASS EXPLOSION DRILL

Denny Stolz
Alma College, Michigan State University, Bowling Green State University,
San Diego State University

Objective: To teach and practice the proper fundamentals and techniques of executing the pass block.

Equipment Needed: Three boards (4' x 12" x 2")

Description:

- Position three boards two yards apart and perpendicular to a selected line of scrimmage.

- Position offensive linemen in two-point stances at the left of each of the boards. A defensive lineman (pass rusher) straddles each board in three-point stances (see diagram).

- Other drill participants stand adjacent to drill area.

- On coach's cadence and snap count, the offensive linemen move from their two-point stances as the pass rushers move forward out of their three-point stances.

- All offensive linemen step across their boards with their onside foot. They extend their arms from the hip to a *lock-out* position and contact the defenders in the pectoral area. The defensive players step and grab the offensive linemen's shoulder pads. Now all drill participants step back to their original positions and description is repeated until the whistle blows.

- Drill continues until all offensive linemen have had a sufficient number of repetitions from both the left and right sides of the board.

Coaching Points:

- Instruct offensive linemen not to overextend themselves. (Their hips should be low and their heads back and up.)

- Make sure that all offensive linemen keep their feet shoulder-width apart at all times.

- Make sure that when linemen execute their *lock-out* techniques that their arms lock-out as they contact the defender and not before.

- Insist that all linemen maintain the proper pass-blocking body position throughout the drill.

- Make sure all linemen practice the proper fundamentals and techniques in executing all pass blocks.

Safety Considerations:

- Proper warm-up should precede drill.

- The coach should look for and eliminate all unacceptable match-ups as to size and athletic ability.

- Maintain a minimum distance of two yards between each board.

- The drill should progress from form blocking to live blocking.

- The coach should monitor closely the intensity of the drill.

- Boards should be beveled and checked for splinters daily.

Variations:

- Can be used as a form or live pass blocking drill.

- Can vary the number of steps and *punches* to simulate the timing of various quarterbacks pass drops.

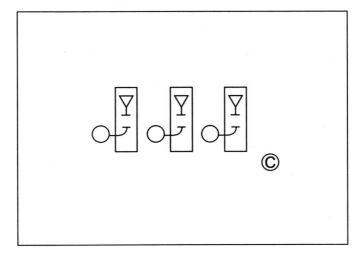

PULLING FOOTWORK DRILL

Charles R. "Chuck" Stobart
Ohio State University, University of Southern California, University of Arizona, University of Pittsburgh, University of Michigan, Miami University (Ohio), Marshall University, University of Toledo, University of Utah, University of Memphis

Objective: To teach and practice the proper fundamentals and techniques of pulling. Special emphasis is placed on footwork.

Equipment Needed: None

Description:

- Align offensive linemen in their stances four yards apart on a selected line of scrimmage. The coach is positioned in front of the drill participants.

- The drill is conducted in five phases as follows:
    - Push-off backward. On coach's cadence and snap count, all linemen push off backward with their down hand. Repeat several times.
    - Thrust elbow back. On coach's cadence and snap count, all linemen push off backward with their down hand thrusting the elbow back and planting the lead (onside) foot in the direction of the pull. Repeat several times both left and right.
    - Lead foot and take-off foot. On coach's cadence and snap count, the preceding phases are repeated placing special emphasis on the lead (onside) and take-off (backside) foot positions. The take-off foot must push and pivot ending up parallel with the lead foot. Repeat both left and right several times.
    - One running step. On coach's cadence and ball snap, all preceding phases are repeated incorporating one running step. Repeat several times both left and right.
    - The pull. On coach's cadence and snap count, all linemen follow the preceding step progression and pull a designated distance. Repeat several times both left and right.

- Drill continues until all offensive linemen have executed a sufficient number of repetitions of all the phases of the drill.

Coaching Points:

- Always check to see that all offensive linemen are in their proper stances.

- Make sure linemen execute each phase of the drill correctly before moving on to the next phase.

- Instruct pulling linemen as to the principle of the pulling curve.

- Make sure all linemen practice the proper fundamentals and techniques incorporated with all phases of the drill.

Safety Considerations:

- Proper warm-up should precede drill.

- Drill area should be clear of all foreign articles.

- The drill should progress from half speed to full speed.

- Maintain a minimum distance of five yards between drill participants.

Variations:

- Can incorporate defenders *jamming* the pulling linemen as they initiate their pulls.

- Can be used with linemen pulling and executing their blocks.

ONE-MAN SLED DRIVE TECHNIQUE*

Dal Shealy

Baylor University, University of Tennessee, Auburn University, Iowa State University, Mars Hill College, Carson-Newman College, University of Richmond
Fellowship of Christian Athletes: President and CEO

Objective: To teach and practice the proper fundamentals and techniques in the execution of the drive block.

Equipment Needed: One-man blocking sled

Description:

- Position all the offensive linemen in a straight line in front of a one-man blocking sled. The drill is conducted in three phases as follows:
    - *Six-point stance* (on hands and knees with toes curled up under feet). On the coach's cadence and snap count, the first lineman explodes into the pad of the sled with a right-shoulder drive block. Special emphasis should be placed on rolling the hips. The procedure is repeated with all the linemen, in turn, executing both left- and right-shoulder drive blocks.
    - *Four-point stance*. On the coach's cadence and snap count, the first lineman explodes from his stance and executes a right-shoulder block on the pad of the sled. Special emphasis is placed on rolling the hips and forming a power angle with the forearm. The sled is driven five to eight yards. Procedure is repeated with all linemen, in turn, executing both left- and right-shoulder drive blocks.
    - *Three-point stance*. Same as the preceding procedure except all the shoulder-drive blocks are executed from a three-point stance.
- The drill continues until all the linemen have had a sufficient number of repetitions in executing the three phases of the drill.

Coaching Points:

- Always check to see that all the linemen are in their proper stances.
- In contacting the sled, emphasize the importance of rolling the hips and forming the *power angle*.
- Instruct the linemen to keep their shoulders squared to the sled throughout all phases of the drill.

---

*Reprinted with permission from *101 Winning Football Drills: From the Legends of the Game* by Jerry Tolley

- Insist that the linemen maintain a good hitting position with their heads up and feet shoulder-width apart.

- When driving the sled, all the linemen should take short driving steps.

- Make sure the linemen practice the proper fundamentals and techniques in the execution of all shoulder blocks.

Safety Considerations:

- Proper warm-up should precede the drill.

- The drill area should be clear of all foreign articles.

- Helmets should be worn with chinstraps snapped.

- The sled should be checked periodically for possible maintenance and repairs.

Variations:

- Can be used for over-and-up, scoop, reach, and wheel blocks.

- Can align blockers three-yards off sled to simulate blocking on a linebacker.

SHORT TRAP DRILL

Dave McClain (Deceased)
Bowling Green State University, Cornell University, Miami University (Ohio),
University of Kansas, Ohio State University, Ball State University,
University of Wisconsin

Objective: To teach and practice the proper fundamentals and techniques of pulling. Incorporated are skills related to applying the principles of the pulling curve.

Equipment Needed: Six arm pads

Description:

- Align a center and a backside pulling guard in their normal positions on a selected line of scrimmage.

- Place three defenders representing the different angles of the pulling curve to the right of the drill participants. The defenders are positioned on their knees with arm pads on their arms (see diagram).

- Other drill participants stand adjacent to the drill area.

- The coach stands to the backside of the drill area.

- On coach's cadence and snap count, the center drives out of his stance and the guard pulls to execute his trap block as the coach signals one of three defenders to stand.

- The pulling guard then adjusts his pull to trap the designated defender.

- Drill continues until all pulling guards have had a sufficient number of repetitions.

- Drill should be run both left and right.

Coaching Points:

- Check to see that all pulling guards are aligned correctly and are in their proper stances.

- Instruct pulling guards as to the principles of the pulling curve.

- Instruct the centers to drive out of their stances so the pulling guards can get a feel for the play.

- Make sure all pulling guards practice the proper fundamentals and techniques of pulling.

Safety Considerations:

- Proper warm-up should precede drill.

- Drill area should be clear of all foreign articles.

- The drill should progress from walk-through to full speed.

- The coach should monitor closely the intensity of the drill.

- Instruct all pulling guards as to the proper fundamentals and techniques of pulling and blocking.

- A quick whistle is imperative with this drill.

Variations:

- Can incorporate other offensive personnel.

- Can be used with various traps and *kick out* plays.

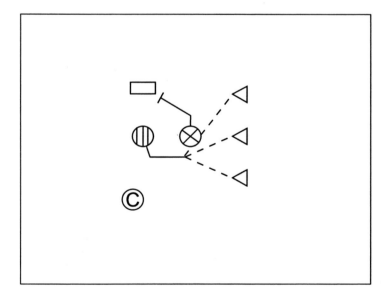

TRIANGLE DRILL

Richard L. Brooks

Oregon State University, University of California at Los Angeles, Los Angeles Rams, San Francisco 49ers, University of Oregon, St. Louis Rams, Atlanta Falcons, University of Kentucky
National Coach of the Year: University of Oregon 1994

Objective: To teach and practice the proper fundamentals and techniques in the execution of center-guard combination blocks. Included are the cutoff-scoop block, the drive-double team block, and the long pull-reach or search block as shown in diagrams.

Equipment Needed: None

Description:

- Align a quarterback, center, and two guards in their normal positions over the football on a selected line of scrimmage.

- Position two linebackers and a nose guard in a 5-2 alignment over the offense.

- Other drill participants stand adjacent to drill area.

- On quarterback's cadence and ball snap, the offense executes designated blocking schemes as the defenders read, react to, and defeat their blocks.

- The blocking schemes can either be called in the huddle or can be signaled by the coach standing behind the defense.

- Drill continues until all offensive linemen have had a sufficient number of repetitions.

- All blocking schemes should be conducted both left and right.

Coaching Points:

- Always check to see that all offensive linemen are aligned correctly and are in their proper stances.

- Make sure all offensive personnel carry out their blocking assignments correctly.

- Make sure all offensive linemen practice the proper fundamentals and techniques related to their specific blocks.

Safety Considerations:

- Proper warm-up should precede drill.
- The drill should progress from half speed to full speed (not live).
- The coach should monitor closely the intensity of the drill.

Variations:

- Can be used with a variety of blocking schemes.
- Can be used against various defensive fronts.
- Can be used as a nose guard or linebacker drill.

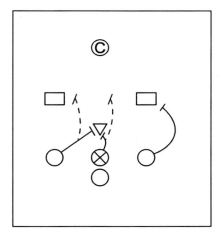

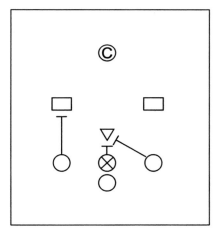

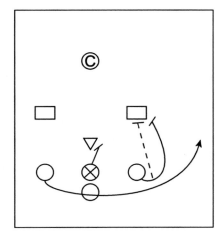

PULL FOR SWEEP*

William G. "Bill" Dooley
Mississippi State University, George Washington University, University of Georgia, University of North Carolina, Virginia Polytechnic Institute and State University, Wake Forest University

Objective: To teach and practice the proper fundamentals and techniques of pulling. Incorporated are skills related to agility, body control, reaction, and quickness.

Equipment Needed: Five cones, four hand shields, and footballs

Description:

- Place five cones—one each at the noseguard, guard, and tackle positions—on a selected line of scrimmage. Position two linebackers and two defensive ends, holding hand shields, in their regular alignments (see diagram).

- Align two offensive guards in their normal positions.

- A tailback, holding a football, is positioned six-yards deep in the backfield.

- Other drill participants stand adjacent to drill area.

- On the coach's cadence and snap count, the offensive personnel execute a designated sweep play utilizing various pulling schemes.

- The defenders react and move according to their basic sweep reads.

- The drill continues until all drill participants have run a sufficient number of repetitions.

- The drill should be run from both left and right formations and from various field positions.

Coaching Points:

- Always check to see that all the drill participants are aligned correctly and are in their proper stances.

- In the execution of the *step-out*, make sure that all linemen pull their onside arm back hard, keeping the elbow as close to the hip as possible.

- Instruct pulling linemen to look for their defenders on their first step.

- Instruct linemen as to the principles of the pulling curve.

*Reprinted with permission from *101 Winning Football Drills: From the Legends of the Game* by Jerry Tolley

- Make sure the linemen use the proper fundamentals and techniques of pulling and blocking.

- Insist that the tailbacks read the defensive end correctly so the linebackers will be in the correct positions for the blocks by the pulling linemen.

Safety Considerations:

- Proper warm-up should precede the drill.

- The drill area should be clear of all foreign articles.

- The drill should progress from half speed to full speed.

- The coach should monitor closely the intensity of the drill.

- Instruct the linemen as to the proper fundamentals and techniques of pulling and blocking.

- Review the different pulling schemes with the defenders and remind them to remain alert.

Variations:

- Can be used as a form or live pulling-and-blocking drill.

- Can incorporate other offensive personnel.

- Can be used for lead and kick-out plays.

- Can be used as a defensive end and linebacker drill.

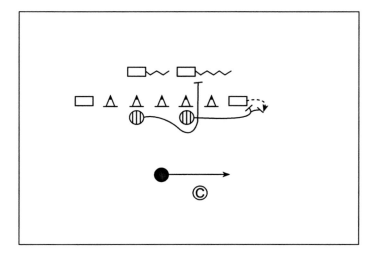

TWO-STEP EXPLOSION

Warren A. Powers
University of Nebraska, Washington State University, University of Missouri
National Coach of the Year: Missouri 1978

Objective: To teach and practice the proper techniques and fundamentals in the execution of the drive block from both left-foot and right-foot starts.

Equipment Needed: Blocking chute (seven stalls—36" high x 48"wide), seven boards (6' x 14" x 2"), and seven large blocking dummies

Description:

- Place a board in each of the starting stalls of a blocking chute.

- Align offensive linemen (center, two guards, and two tackles) in waves behind the stalls of the blocking chute.

- Position a defender holding a large blocking dummy in front of each blocking stall.

- On coach's command, the first wave of offensive linemen takes their stances under the chutes.

- On coach's cadence and snap count, linemen drive off their right foot and take the first two steps in executing a drive block on the defender. Description is repeated with left-foot starts.

- Drill continues until all offensive linemen have had a sufficient number of repetitions with both left-and right-foot starts.

Coaching Points:

- Always check to see that offensive linemen are aligned correctly and are in their proper stances.

- Make sure all linemen's first steps are quick and short (four to six inches).

- Instruct all linemen to direct their aiming points on the number area of the defender.

- Instruct linemen to contact the dummy on the *rise* with their heads up, shoulders square to the defender, and their feet shoulder-width apart and driving.

- Make sure all linemen practice the proper fundamentals and techniques of the drive block.

Safety Considerations:

- Proper warm-up should precede drill.
- It is imperative that helmets be worn with chinstraps snapped.
- Boards should be beveled and checked for splinters daily.
- Instruct all offensive linemen as to the proper fundamentals and techniques of the drive block.

BEAR PULLING DRILL

Hanley Hayes Painter (Deceased)
Lenoir-Rhyne College

Objective: To teach and practice the proper fundamentals and techniques of pulling. Incorporated are skills related to stance, body balance, and blocking.

Equipment Needed: Four large blocking dummies and two hand shields

Description:

- Align five interior linemen over the football on a selected line of scrimmage.

- Place four large dummies with holders over the offense. Position a play-side linebacker and a strong safety with hand shields in their regular alignments (see diagram).

- Other drill participants stand adjacent to drill area.

- On coach's cadence and snap count, the entire offensive line executes their blocking assignments on various pulling plays.

- The drill continues until a sufficient number of repetitions have been completed.

- All plays should be run from both left and right formations and from various positions on the field.

Coaching Points:

- Always check to see that all offensive linemen are aligned correctly and are in their proper stances.

- Special emphasis should be placed on the *step-out* technique. (Pulling linemen take a short and slightly backward step with onside foot by *whipping* elbow backward across onside knee. The *off* hand touches the ground at the point where the onside foot was first positioned.)

- Instruct pulling linemen as to the principles of the pulling curve.

- Make sure all offensive linemen practice the proper fundamentals and techniques of pulling.

Safety Considerations:

- Proper warm-up should precede drill.

- Drill area should be clear of all foreign articles.

- The drill should progress from walk-through to full speed.

- The coach should monitor closely the intensity of the drill.

- Instruct all pulling linemen as to the proper fundamentals and techniques of pulling and blocking.

Variations:

- Can be used as a form and live pulling and blocking drill.

- Can be used against various defensive alignments.

- Can be used as a defensive drill.

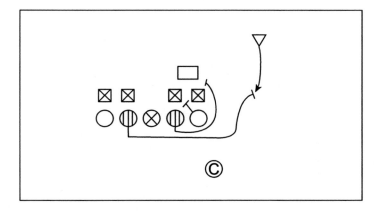

BLITZ PICKUP

Jimmye M. Laycock
Clemson University, University of Memphis, The Citadel,
The College of William and Mary

Objective: To teach and practice the proper fundamentals and techniques of reading and blocking various blitzing schemes.

Equipment Needed: Seven hand shields and footballs

Description:

- Align an offensive unit over the football on a selected line of scrimmage.

- Position a defensive front, holding hand shields, over the offense (see diagram).

- Alternating units stand adjacent to drill area.

- On cadence and ball snap, the offense executes various pass actions (three-step, five-step, seven-step, sprint, play action, etc).

- The defenders react to the ball snap and run the various blitzes used by the upcoming opponents. (On Monday and Thursday, review opponent's two favorite blitzes. On Tuesday and Wednesday, review other stunts.)

- Drill continues until all units have had a sufficient number of repetitions.

- Drill should be run from both left and right formations.

Coaching Points:

- Always check to see that all offensive personnel are aligned correctly and are in their proper stances.

- Make sure all offensive linemen carry out their proper assignment against the various blitzes.

- Make sure all linemen practice the proper fundamentals and techniques of pass blocking.

- Insist that the drill be conducted at full speed.

Safety Considerations:

- It is imperative that proper warm-up precede drill.
- Drill area should be clear of all foreign articles.
- The coach should watch for and eliminate all unacceptable matchups as to size and athletic ability.
- Instruct all blitzing personnel to stop their blitzes when *fronted* by a blocker.
- The coach should monitor closely the intensity of the drill.

Variations:

- Can be used without defenders holding shields.
- Can be used as a form or live drill.
- Can be used as a defensive drill.

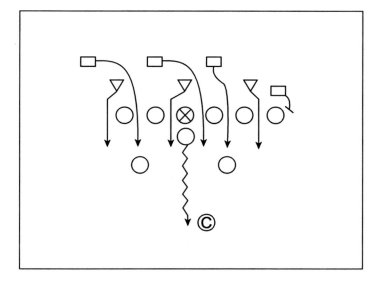

BLOCKING PROGRESSION (EXPLOSION) DRILL

Frederick H. "Fred" Dunlap
University of Buffalo, Cornell University, Lehigh University, Colgate University

Objective: To teach and practice the proper fundamentals and techniques in the execution of the shoulder block.

Equipment Needed: Seven-man sled

Description:

- Align seven offensive linemen in front of the pads of a seven-man sled. Other linemen fall in behind the front line.

- On coach's command all linemen execute two right and two left shoulder blocks (in rhythm) as outlined in the following four phases.

  - Six-point stance. (On hands and knees and with toes curled up under feet.) On coach's command, linemen *explode* into the pad of the sled delivering a right shoulder block while extending the hips as far forward as possible. This should put all linemen in a front lying position. Linemen return to their six-point stances and on command the technique is repeated once more with the right shoulder and then twice with the left shoulder.

  - Two-point stance. On coach's command, linemen step with their right foot and then deliver right shoulder blows to the pads of the sled. (Left foot remains planted when stepping with right foot.) Technique is repeated as in the six-point stance description.

  - Three-point stance. On coach's command, linemen step with the left foot first and then step with right foot delivering a blow to the pad of the sled with the right shoulder technique is repeated as in the two-point stance description.

  - Three-point stance and drive. Same as in the three-point stance description, except that after the shoulder blocks are executed, the linemen drive the sled until the coach blows his whistle.

- Drill continues until all linemen have had a sufficient number of repetitions in executing the four phases.

Coaching Points:

- Always check to see that linemen are in their designated stances.

- Instruct linemen to concentrate on an aiming point one yard behind the pad.

- In contacting the pad, make sure the arm is bent to form a 90-degree blocking surface angle with the wrist rotated inward.

- Instruct linemen to keep their shoulders *square* to the pad of the sled throughout all phases of the drill.

- Insist that linemen maintain good hitting positions with the head up and feet shoulder-width apart.

- When driving the sled, all linemen should take short driving steps.

- Make sure the linemen practice the proper fundamentals and techniques in the execution of all shoulder blocks.

Safety Considerations:

- Proper warm-up should precede drill.

- Helmets should be worn with chinstraps snapped.

- The sled should be checked periodically for possible maintenance and repairs.

BOARD BLOCKING

Nick Coso
Eastern Michigan University, Kent State University, Ferris State College

Objective: To teach and practice the proper fundamentals and techniques in the execution of the drive block.

Equipment Needed: Board (6' x 10' x 2") and a large blocking dummy

Description:
- Place a board perpendicular to a selected line of scrimmage.
- Align an offensive lineman in a three-point stance straddling the midpoint of the board.
- Position a defender holding a dummy in a straddling position over the board and across from the offensive lineman.
- Other drill participants stand adjacent to the drill area.
- On coach's cadence and snap count, the offensive lineman explodes out of his stance and executes a drive block on the defender driving him off the end of the board.
- The defender reacts to the movement of the offensive lineman and takes a step forward and resists his block.
- Drill continues until all offensive linemen have had a sufficient number of repetitions.

Coaching Points:
- Always check to see that all offensive linemen are in their proper stances.
- Instruct linemen to contact the dummy on the rise with heads up, shoulders squared to the defender, and feet shoulder-width apart and driving.
- Make sure all offensive linemen practice the proper fundamentals and techniques of the drive block.

Safety Considerations:
- Proper warm-up should precede drill.
- The drill should progress from half speed to full speed.
- The coach should monitor closely the intensity of the drill.
- The boards should be beveled and checked for splinters daily.
- Instruct linemen as to the proper fundamentals and techniques of the drive block.

MONSTER DRILL

J. Pete Murray
Texas A&I University

Objective: To teach and practice the proper fundamentals and techniques of the drive block.

Equipment Needed: Blocking chute (seven stalls—54" high x 48" wide), seven boards (6' x 10" x 2"), and seven large blocking dummies

Description:
- Place one board in each of the starting stalls of the blocking chute. The boards should extend beyond the front of the stalls.
- Align offensive linemen in waves behind the stalls of the blocking chute.
- Position a defender holding a dummy in front of each blocking stall. Defenders stand straddling the boards so dummies can be placed just under the blocking stalls. Dummy holders are instructed to resist the blocks of the offensive linemen.
- On coach's cadence and snap count, the first wave of offensive linemen drive from their stances and execute drive blocks on the defenders.
- Offensive linemen continue to drive the dummy holder back until the defender is pushed off the end of the board.
- Drill continues until all linemen have had a sufficient number of repetitions.

Coaching Points:
- Make sure all linemen are aligned correctly and are in their proper stances.
- Instruct linemen to contact the dummy on the *rise* with their heads up, shoulders *square* to the defender and feet shoulder-width apart and driving.
- Make sure all linemen practice the proper fundamentals and techniques of the drive block.

Safety Considerations:
- Proper warm-up should precede drill.
- It is imperative that helmets be worn with chinstraps snapped.
- Boards should be beveled and checked for splinters daily.
- Instruct linemen as to the proper fundamentals and techniques of the drive block.

Variation:
- Can be used with dummies held at the linebacker positions.

LINE PUNCH*

Dennis "Fran" Franchione

Kansas State University, Tennessee Technological University, Texas Christian University, University of New Mexico, Southwest Texas State University, Pittsburg State University, Southwestern College, University of Alabama, Texas A & M University

National Coach of the Year: Pittsburg State 1986 and 1987

Objective: To teach and practice the proper fundamentals in executing the punch technique in pass blocking.

Equipment Needed: Five-man or seven-man blocking sled

Description:

- Align a row of offensive linemen adjacent and parallel to a five- or seven-man blocking sled. All the linemen are facing the sled (see diagram).

- On the coach's command, the first lineman slides in front of the first sled pad and executes the *punch* technique. He then slides laterally to the second sled pad and executes another *punch* technique. He continues until he has executed the *punch* technique on each sled pad.

- When the first lineman has completed his slide through and *punching*, the second lineman takes his turn, etc.

- The drill continues until all the linemen have had a sufficient number of repetitions moving from both the left and the right on the sled.

Coaching Points:

- Instruct the linemen as to the proper fundamentals and techniques of executing the *punch* technique.

- Make sure the linemen focus on the target area of the pad as they execute the *punch*.

- Emphasize that the speed of the slide between the pads is not as important as the execution of the punch.

- Insist that the linemen maintain a good *punching* position with their head up, eyes focused on the target area, and feet shoulder-width apart as they slide from one pad to another.

---

*Reprinted with permission from 101 Winning Football Drills: From the Legends of the Game by Jerry Tolley

Safety Considerations:

- Proper warm-up should precede the drill.

- The sled should be checked periodically for possible maintenance and repairs.

- The drill should progress from formwork to full speed.

Variation:

- Can be used with a row of defenders aligned facing the offensive linemen. Drill participants should be two-feet apart and the offensive linemen should be instructed to step forward as they executes the *punch* technique on the forward-stepping defender.

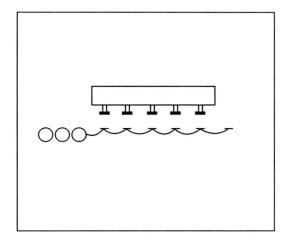

3

Center Drills

BLAST AND BEWILDER

Richard Bruce Craddock (Deceased)
Truman State University, University of Vermont, Western Illinois University

Objective: To teach and practice the proper fundamentals and techniques of the center-quarterback ball exchange and the execution of the drive block.

Equipment Needed: Blocking chute, board (24" x 18"), one-man blocking sled, and a football

Description:

- Position a center over a football in a stall of a blocking chute.

- A one-man blocking sled is aligned twenty-four inches in front of the stall. The board is placed between the blocking chute and sled (see diagram).

- A quarterback is positioned over the center.

- Other drill participants stand adjacent to the drill area.

- On quarterback's cadence, the center snaps the football, drives out of his stance, straddles the board, and executes a right shoulder drive block on the sled. The sled is driven 10 yards upfield.

- Drill continues until all centers have executed a sufficient number of both left and right shoulder drive blocks.

Coaching Points:

- Always check to see that centers are in their proper stances.

- Make sure the center-quarterback exchange is executed correctly.

- Instruct the centers to drive out low and hard. They should contact the sled on the *rise* with their heads up, shoulders *square* to the sled and their feet shoulder-width apart and driving.

- Make sure all centers practice the proper fundamentals and techniques of the drive block.

Safety Considerations:

- Proper warm-up should precede drill.
- The board should be beveled and checked for splinters daily.
- The sled should be checked periodically for possible maintenance and repairs.
- It is imperative that helmets be worn with chinstraps snapped.
- Instruct the centers as to the proper fundamentals and techniques of executing the shoulder drive block and hitting the sled.

Variations:

- Can be used with a defender holding a dummy in front of the chute.
- Can be used as an offensive line drill.
- Can be used as a center-quarterback ball exchange drill.

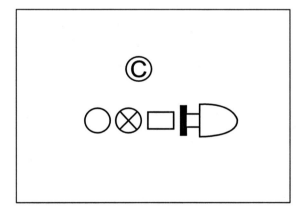

BLOCKING LINEBACKERS

Lonnie "Mack" Carden Elon University

Objective: To teach and practice the proper fundamentals and techniques in blocking fast *flow* linebackers.

Equipment Needed: Three large blocking dummies and footballs

Description:

- Align three defenders (linebackers) holding dummies (large ends up) five yards apart and five yards upfield from a selected line of scrimmage.
- Stagger three centers over footballs five yards to the left of the dummies (linebackers) on the selected line of scrimmage (see diagram).
- Position quarterbacks over the centers.
- The coach stands adjacent to the drill area.
- On a designated quarterback's cadence, the centers snap the football and step at a 45-degree angle to the right and toward the linebackers.
- On their third step, the centers turn upfield and execute drive blocks on the dummies (linebackers).
- Drill continues until all centers have had a sufficient number of repetitions.
- Drill should be conducted both left and right.

Coaching Points:

- Always check to see that centers are in their proper stances.
- Make sure the center-quarterback exchange is executed property.
- Instruct the centers to drive off the football at a 45-degree angle and to turn upfield after the third step.
- Make sure all centers practice the proper fundamentals and techniques in the execution of the shoulder drive block.

Safety Considerations:

- Proper warm-up should precede drill.

- Make sure a minimum distance of five yards is maintained between each of the centers and each of the dummies.

- Instruct the centers as to the proper fundamentals and techniques of executing the drive block.

- Instruct holders to hold dummies firmly as the drive blocks are being executed.

Variations:

- Can be used with three additional dummies placed 10 yards downfield to block for second effort.

- Can be used as an offensive line drill.

- Can be used as a center-quarterback ball exchange drill.

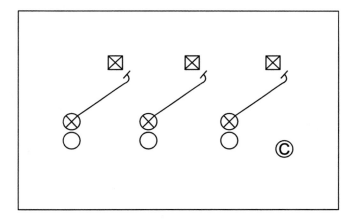

CENTER FOLDS AND PULLS

Paul Schudel
University of New Hampshire, Colorado State University,
The College of William and Mary, Syracuse University, University of Michigan,
Ball State University, University of Illinois, University of Virginia,
Central Connecticut State University

Objective: To teach and practice the proper fundamentals and techniques of pulling behind the line of scrimmage and moving through any gap to block a linebacker.

Equipment Needed: Six cones, six large blocking dummies, and footballs

Description:

- Align cones at the offensive guards, tackles, and tight ends positions on a selected line of scrimmage.

- Lay blocking dummies across from and perpendicular to the line of scrimmage and in front of each of the cones (see diagram).

- A center, quarterback, and tailback take their normal positions over the football.

- A linebacker is aligned in his regular position.

- Other centers stand adjacent to drill area.

- On quarterback's cadence, the offense executes a designated play as the linebacker pursues the ballcarrier.

- The center pulls or folds (depending on the linebacker's pursuit) and executes his normal base block on the linebacker.

- Drill continues until all centers have had a sufficient number of pulls or folds both from the left and the right.

Coaching Points:

- Always check to see that centers are aligned correctly and are in their proper stances.

- Make sure the centers' first step is taken laterally and not upfield.

- Instruct the centers to turn their shoulders as they pull and then to square them again as they cross the line of scrimmage to execute their block on the linebacker.

Safety Considerations:

- It is imperative that proper warm-up precede drill.

- The drill should progress from form work to full speed.

- The coach should monitor closely the intensity of the drill.

- This is not a live blocking and tackling drill.

- A quick whistle is imperative with this drill.

Variations:

- Can be used without a ballcarrier with the coach designating the pursuit route of the linebackers.

- Can be used with offensive linemen and a complete defensive front (live blocking, no tackling).

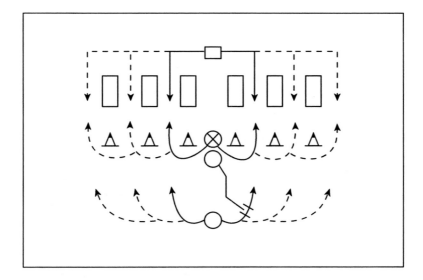

CENTER PASS BLOCKING

Larry M. Wilcox
Benedictine College

Objectives: To teach and practice the proper fundamentals and techniques of pass blocking. Incorporated are skills related to balance, quickness, and agility.

Equipment Needed: Two large blocking dummies and footballs

Description:

- Align a center and quarterback over the football on a selected line of scrimmage.
- Position a nose guard over the center.
- Lay two blocking dummies at a 45-degree angle from the line of scrimmage (see diagram).
- Other centers stand adjacent to drill area.
- On quarterback's cadence, the center snaps the football and executes his pass block on the on rushing nose guard. The quarterback takes his normal seven-step pass drop.
- The drill ends either when the center has executed his block properly or the nose guard has touched the quarterback.
- Drill continues until all centers have had a sufficient number of repetitions.

Coaching Points:

- Always check to see that centers are aligned correctly and are in their proper stances.
- Make sure the center-quarterback ball exchange is executed correctly.
- Instruct the centers to *slide* their feet while maintaining a *squared* relationship to the line of scrimmage. The head should be up, knees bent, and the heels should be off the ground.
- Insist that centers always maintain a position between the nose guard and quarterback.
- Make sure the centers always know the quarterback's pass drop pattern.

Safety Considerations:

- It is imperative that proper warm-up precede drill.
- Drill area should be cleared of all foreign articles.
- The coach should look for and eliminate all unacceptable match-ups as to size and athletic ability.
- The drill should progress from form blocking to live blocking.
- The coach should monitor closely the intensity of the drill.
- Instruct centers never to cut block the nose guard.

Variations:

- Can be used as a form or live blocking drill.
- Can be used as a nose guard pass rushing drill.
- Can be used as a center-quarterback ball exchange drill.

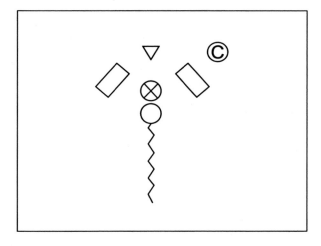

EXPLOSION LUNGE-STEP DRILL

Fred A. Zechman
Ohio State University, Youngstown State University, New Mexico State University

Objective: To teach and practice the proper fundamentals and techniques of executing the drive block. Can also be used as a center-quarterback ball exchange drill.

Equipment Needed: Two boards (10' x 2' x 2"), one large blocking dummy, and footballs

Description:

- Place one board in a horizontal position on a selected line of scrimmage. Place another board at the midpoint and perpendicular to the first board. A defender, holding a blocking dummy, is positioned straddling the perpendicular board and twelve inches from the line of scrimmage (see diagram).

- A quarterback and center are aligned over a football in front of the defender. The center's feet are positioned six inches behind the horizontal board.

- Other drill participants stand adjacent to the drill area.

- On quarterback's cadence, the center snaps the football and takes a short step to the near edge of the horizontal board. The backside foot now steps across the horizontal board as the center executes a drive block on the defender holding the dummy.

- The center now drives the defender off the end of the board.

- Drill continues until all centers have had a sufficient number of repetitions.

Coaching Points:

- Always check to see that centers are in their proper stances.

- Make sure the center-quarterback ball exchange is executed correctly.

- Instruct the centers to contact the dummy on the *rise* with their heads up, shoulders *squared* to the defender, and their feet shoulder-width apart and driving.

- Insist that the centers always drive the head to the play-side of the dummy.

- Make sure all centers practice the proper fundamentals and techniques of the drive block.

Safety Considerations:

- Proper warm-up should precede drill.

- Board should be beveled and checked for splinters daily.

- The drill should progress from form work to full speed.

- The coach should monitor closely the intensity of the drill.

- Instruct all linemen as to the proper fundamentals and techniques of the drive block.

Variations:

- Can be used with the perpendicular board placed in an offset position to the horizontal board to simulate a *shade* nose guard. Perpendicular board can be placed at a 45-degree angle to simulate blocking a linebacker.

- Can be used as an offensive line drill.

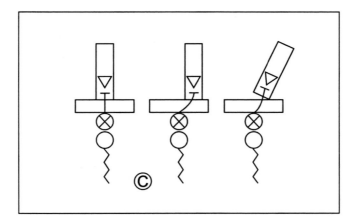

REACH BLOCK DRILL

John D. McCann
Southwest Texas State University, McNeese State University

Objective: To teach and practice the proper fundamentals and techniques in the execution of the reach block. Incorporated are skills related to agility, flexibility, and quickness.

Equipment Needed: A large blocking dummy and footballs

Description:

- Position a center and quarterback over the football on a selected line of scrimmage.
- Align a defender holding a dummy (nose guard) in a shade position over the center.
- Other centers stand adjacent to drill area.
- On quarterback's cadence, the center snaps the football and executes the reach block on the dummy (*shade* nose guard).
- Drill continues until all centers have had a sufficient number of repetitions.
- Drill should be run with the defender aligned at both a left and right *shade* position to the center.

Coaching Points:

- Always check to see that the centers are aligned correctly and are in their proper stances.
- Make sure center-quarterback ball exchange is executed correctly.
- Instruct centers to step with their play-side foot first and to keep their shoulders *square* to the line of scrimmage.
- Make sure all centers practice the proper fundamentals and techniques of the reach block.

Safety Considerations:

• Proper warm-up should precede drill.

• The drill should progress from form work to full speed.

• The coach should monitor closely the intensity of the drill.

• Instruct all centers as to the proper fundamentals and techniques of the reach block.

Variations:

• Can be used as a form or live blocking drill.

• Can be used with defender lined up head up the play-side guard.

• Can be used as an offensive line drill.

• Can be used as a center-quarterback ball exchange drill.

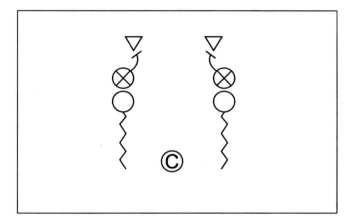

REFINING THE SCOOP TECHNIQUE

Michael L. "Mike" Turner
Lees McRae College, Catawba College, University of North Alabama,
Carson-Newman College
National Assistant Coach of the Year: Carson-Newman 2003

Objective: To teach and practice the proper fundamentals and techniques in the execution of the scoop block

Equipment Needed: Large blocking dummy, hand shield, and a football

Description:

- Position a center and quarterback over the football on a selected line of scrimmage.

- Align a nose guard and a backside linebacker in their normal defensive positions. The nose guard holds a dummy and the linebacker holds a hand shield.

- Other centers stand adjacent to drill area.

- The coach stands play-side and instructs the defensive personnel as to the charge to take (see diagram).

- On quarterback's cadence, the center snaps the football and steps to the play-side gap at a 45-degree angle using at least three *crab* technique steps. If the nose guard charges play-side gap, the center is instructed to block him. If after the third *crab* technique step the center has not made contact with the nose guard, he clears the line of scrimmage and blocks the linebacker.

- Drill continues until all centers have had a sufficient number of repetitions.

- Drill should be run both left and right.

Coaching Points:

- Always check to see that centers are in their proper stances.

- Make sure the center-quarterback ball exchange is executed correctly.

- Instruct centers always to step at a 45-degree angle to the play-side as they snap the football.

- Remind the backside linebackers to react to the play-side gap.

- Make sure all centers practice the proper fundamentals and techniques of the *scoop* block.

Safety Considerations:

- Proper warm-up should precede drill.

- The drill should progress from form work to full speed.

- The coach should monitor closely the intensity of the drill.

- Instruct all centers as to the proper fundamentals and techniques of the *scoop* block.

Variations:

- Can be used as a form or live blocking drill.

- Can be used as a nose guard and linebacker drill.

- Can be used as a center-quarterback ball exchange drill.

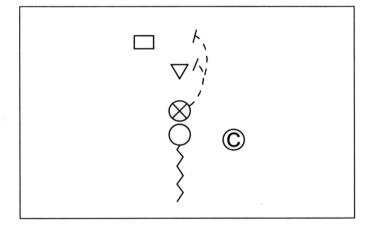

4

Quarterback Ball Handling and Passing Drills

SPRINT OUT PASS DRILL

Paul Hamilton
The Citadel, Wofford College, United States Air Force Academy,
East Tennessee State University, Elon University

Objective: To teach and practice the proper mechanics of passing the football in the execution of sprint out passes. Special attention is paid to the sprint-out path taken by the quarterbacks.

Equipment Needed: Six cones and footballs

Description:

- Position a center on a selected line of scrimmage on each hash mark. Place three cones, in a slight angle and parallel row, to the selected line of scrimmage and on the field-side of the centers. The cone placement will ensure that the quarterbacks' initial sprint-side steps will gain for them the appropriate depth (see diagram).

- Align a receiver five yards from each sideline and five yards downfield from the selected line of scrimmage.

- Alternating quarterbacks stand adjacent to the drill area or may serve as centers.

- The coach stands behind the drill area.

- On coach's command, the designated quarterback aligns himself under the center on the left hash mark; he calls the cadence and on ball snap sprints to his right, around the cones, and passes the football to the stationary receiver standing adjacent to the right sideline.

- The same quarterback will immediately align himself under the center on the right hash mark and the drill is repeated with the quarterback sprinting to his left.

- The same quarterback repeats descriptions five and six once again.

- The drill continues until all quarterbacks have had a sufficient number of repetitions.

Coaching Points:

- Always check to see that quarterbacks are in their proper stances.

- Instruct the quarterbacks to always open with the play-side foot and to gain depth when taking their initial step from under the center.

- Make sure quarterbacks have the football in the *pass ready* position on their third-to-fifth step and to always have their eyes focused downfield on the receiver.

- Insist that quarterbacks have their shoulders *squared* to the receiver when the football is released.

- Instruct the quarterbacks to finish the throw as if they were sprinting to the receiver.

- Make sure all quarterbacks practice the proper mechanics in throwing all passes.

Safety Considerations:

- Proper warm-up should precede drill.

- Drill area (including sideline areas) should be clear of all foreign articles.

Variations:

- Can be used with receivers positioned at various spots on the field to simulate other pass route ending points.

- Can be used with quarterback taking the snap from the shotgun formation.

- Can position two receivers at various pass route ending positions and present quarterbacks with a *read key* for horizontal or vertical progression (e.g., flat-curl, flat-corner).

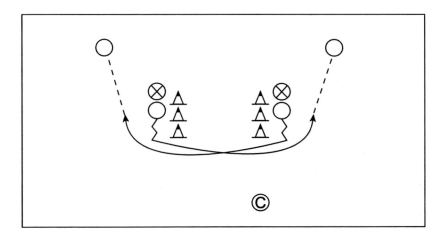

QUARTERBACK CONE SHUFFLE DRILL

Jeff Bower
University of Southern Mississippi, Southern Methodist University,
Wake Forest University, Oklahoma State University

Objective: To teach and practice the proper mechanics of passing the football. Incorporated are skills related to lateral movement and releasing the quick pass while moving in the pocket.

Equipment Needed: Six cones and footballs (passing net optional)

Description:

- Place six cones in a row perpendicular to a selected line of scrimmage. The cones are placed at a 45-degree angle from one another and are separated in both width and depth by two yards (see diagram).

- Align a row of quarterbacks in a pass drop position behind the deepest cone.

- A receiver is positioned 10 yards downfield and in front of the first cone.

- The coach is positioned adjacent to the receiver.

- The first quarterback, at a deliberate speed, *shuffles and weaves* through the cones and releases the *quick* pass to the receivers as he works through the last cone.

- When the first quarterback releases his *quick* pass, the second quarterback begins his *shuffle* and *weaves* through the cones and throws his pass. This phase of the drill continues until all quarterbacks have completed *shuffling* and *weaving* through the cones and throwing the pass to the receiver.

- The drill continues with the quarterbacks *working* their way through the cones and passing the football to a receiver aligned 10 yards deep and both five yards to the left and right of the front cone.

- In the final phase of the drill, the receiver is again positioned 10 yards in front of the first cone. This time, when the quarterback is in the middle of his *shuffle* and *weave*, the coach yells "Now," and the quarterback releases the ball on the *now* command.

Coaching Points:

- When the quarterbacks move through the cones, emphasize the importance of the quarterbacks always being under control.

- Instruct the quarterbacks to always have the football in the proper *carriage* position with the football held high on the numbers and on the side of the throwing arm.

- As the quarterbacks *feel* their way through the cones, insist that their knees are slightly bent and the eyes are focused on the receiver.
- Instruct the quarterbacks to avoid crossover stepping and to always plant the outside foot when changing directions.
- Emphasize the importance of releasing the pass quickly.
- Make sure all quarterbacks practice the proper mechanics in throwing all passes.

Safety Considerations:

- Proper warm-up should precede drill.
- Drill area should be clear of all foreign articles.

Variations:

- Can be used with a passing net.
- Can be used with eight cones.
- Can be used with cones spaced at wider and deeper alignments.
- Can be used with the quarterbacks *shuffling* and *weaving* through the cones at full speed.

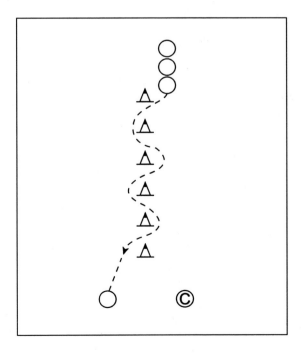

CIRCLE DRILL*

The Honorable Dr. Thomas "Tom" Osborne
University of Nebraska
National Champions: 1994, 1995, and 1997
National Coach of the Year: 1978, 1983, 1994, and 1995
Fellowship of Christian Athletes Grant Teaff Coach of the Year: 1997
College Football Hall of Fame: 1998
Amos Alonzo Stagg Award: 2000

Objective: To teach and practice the proper mechanics of passing a football while running in a circle. Special emphasis is placed on maintaining the correct body alignment.

Equipment Needed: Footballs

Description:

- Align paired quarterbacks with a football 15-yards apart as shown in the diagram.

- On the first command, the paired quarterbacks circle in a counterclockwise direction passing the football back and forth to each other.

- On the second command, the paired quarterbacks change direction and execute their passes while running in a clockwise direction.

- The drill continues until all quarterbacks have thrown a sufficient number of passes.

Coaching Points:

- Instruct all the quarterbacks to keep the football above the shoulders as they circle.

- Insist that all the quarterbacks draw their hips and square their shoulders as each pass is thrown.

- Make sure all the quarterbacks practice the proper mechanics in throwing all passes.

*Reprinted with permission from *101 Winning Football Drills: From the Legends of the Game* by Jerry Tolley

Safety Considerations:

- Proper warm-up should precede the drill.

- The drill area should be clear of all foreign articles.

- Maintain a safe distance between each pair of paired drill participants.

Variation:

- Can vary the distance between the paired quarterbacks.

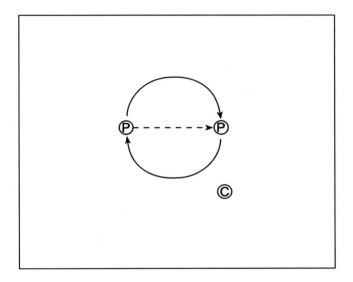

FADE DRILL

Louis "Sonny" Lubick
Montana State University, University of Miami, Stanford University,
Colorado State University
National Coach of the Year: Colorado State 1994

Objective: To teach and practice the proper mechanics of throwing the long pass with special emphasis placed on ball trajectory

Equipment Needed: Footballs

Description:

- Align a quarterback on both sidelines of the football field at the 50-yard line.

- Position a line of receivers on each sideline 15 yards to the right of each quarterback (see diagram).

- Other quarterbacks stand adjacent to sideline areas.

- On quarterback's command, the first receiver in each line runs across the field at three-quarter speed and catches the high trajectory pass thrown by the quarterback.

- After catching the pass, the receiver returns the football to the quarterback on that side of the field and changes receiving line.

- Drill continues until all quarterbacks have thrown a sufficient number of passes.

Coaching Points:

- Stress the importance of releasing the ball on a high trajectory.

- Make sure all quarterbacks practice the proper mechanics in throwing all passes.

Safety Considerations:

- Proper warm-up should precede drill.

- Drill area (including sideline areas) should be clear of all foreign articles.

Variations:

- Can vary the distance receivers line up from quarterbacks.

- Can be used as a wide receiver drill.

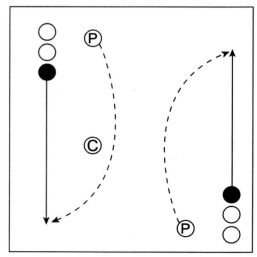

HIGH RELEASE DRILL

Mike Clark
Virginia Military Institute, Virginia Polytechnic Institute and State University, University of Cincinnati, Murray State University, Bridgewater College
National Coach of the Year: Bridgewater 2001

Objective: To teach and practice the proper fundamentals and mechanics of passing the football. Special emphasis is placed on getting the quarterback to *push* the football *up and away* with their throwing motion.

Equipment Needed: "L" Screen (pitcher's net) and footballs

Description:

- Position a quarterback behind the high side of an "L" screen (pitcher's net).

- Position a receiver at a designated distance on the opposite side of the "L" screen.

- Alternating quarterbacks stand adjacent to the drill area.

- The coach is positioned beside the quarterback and observes the passing mechanics of each thrown pass.

- At deliberate speed, the designated quarterback passes the football over the "L" screen to the receiver.

- The receiver catches the football and returns it to the coach who in turn gives it back to the quarterback.

- Drill continues until all quarterbacks have had a sufficient number of repetitions passing the football at different trajectories (*drilled, arc,* and *lob*) to receivers positioned at various distances on the other side of the "L" screen.

Coaching Points:

- Instruct all quarterbacks to *push* the football *up and away* before releasing each pass.

- Emphasize the importance of letting the *natural* throwing motion take over after the football is pushed *up and away*.

- Make sure all quarterbacks practice the proper mechanics in throwing all passes.

Safety Consideration:

- Make sure the quarterback is positioned far enough behind the "L" screen so his throwing arm will not contact the screen during his follow-through.

FLASH DRILL

A. L. Williams
Northwestern State University, Louisiana Tech University
National Coach of the Year: Louisiana Tech 1984

Objective: To teach and practice the proper mechanics of passing the football and reading the open receiver.

Equipment Needed: Footballs

Description:

- Position a quarterback and a center over the football at the midpoint of a selected line of scrimmage.

- Align a receiver on each hash mark eight yards beyond the line of scrimmage. A third receiver is placed in the middle of the field 10 yards beyond the line of scrimmage.

- The coach stands seven yards behind and to the right of the quarterback.

- Other quarterbacks stand adjacent to the drill area or they may serve as receivers.

- On cadence and ball snap, the quarterback initiates his pass drop as he looks at the three receivers.

- On the quarterback's second pass drop step, the coach signals one of the three receivers to *flash* his right hand across his chest.

- Reading the signal, the quarterback passes that receiver the football.

- Drill continues until all quarterbacks have thrown a sufficient number of passes.

- Drill should be run from both the left and right hash marks as well as from midfield.

Coaching Points:

- Always check to see that quarterbacks are in their proper stances.

- Make sure the center-quarterback ball exchange is executed properly.

- Instruct the quarterback to read all three receivers.

- Make sure all quarterbacks practice the proper mechanics in throwing all passes.

Safety Considerations:

- Proper warm-up should precede drill.

- Drill area should be cleared of all foreign articles.

Variations:

- Can be used with various quarterback pass drops and receiver alignments.

- Can be used as a center-quarterback ball exchange drill.

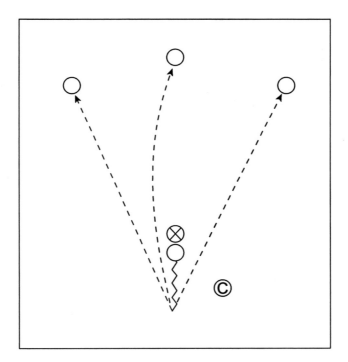

DROP-BACK DRILL*

Jim J. Sweeney
Montana State University, Washington State University, Oakland Raiders,
St. Louis Cardinals, California State University at Fresno

Objective: To teach and practice the proper mechanics in the execution of the three-step, five-step, and seven-step pass drops.

Equipment Needed: Footballs

Description:

- Align a quarterback with a football in a post-snap position on a selected line of scrimmage.

- Other quarterbacks stand adjacent to the drill area.

- The coach stands directly in front of quarterback in a front-facing position.

- On the cadence and snap count, the quarterback executes a three-step pass drop and sets to pass. The quarterback now sprints back to his post-snap alignment and procedure is repeated two more times. This completes the three-step pass-drop set phase of the drill.

- The drill continues, repeating procedure four for the five-step and seven-step pass drops.

- After the third set of seven-step pass drops is completed, the quarterback works his feet in place and the coach signals him to sprint left or right.

- The drill continues until all the quarterbacks have had a sufficient number of repetitions.

Coaching Points:

- Always check to see that the quarterbacks are in their proper stances.

- Make sure all the quarterbacks execute each pass drop correctly.

- Always check for the proper ball position as the quarterback sets to pass.

*Reprinted with permission from *101 Winning Football Drills: From the Legends of the Game* by Jerry Tolley

Safety Consideration:

- Proper warm-up should precede the drill.

Variations:

- Can be used with a center snap.
- Can incorporate all the quarterbacks in the drill at the same time.
- Can have the quarterback pass the football to a receiver after each pass drop.

KNEE DRILL

Robert L. "Bob" Waters (Deceased)
Presbyterian College, Stanford University, Western Carolina University

Objectives: To teach and practice the proper mechanics of gripping and passing the football in a quick throwing motion. Incorporated are skills related to wrist snap and upper-body follow-through.

Equipment Needed: Footballs

Description:

- Align paired quarterbacks in a front-facing position 10 yards apart on their right knees (right handed). Five yards should separate each pair of paired quarterbacks.

- Footballs with laces away are placed in front of the right knee (right handed) of one of each of the paired quarterbacks.

- At deliberate pace, quarterbacks pick up the footballs with both hands and position them under their chins.

- The quarterbacks now move the footballs to their right ears (right-handed) and release pass as quickly as possible aiming for their partners' facemasks.

- Passes should be thrown with enough velocity so that the passers will have to catch themselves on the ground with the throwing hand.

- Drill continues until all paired quarterbacks have had a sufficient number of repetitions.

Coaching Points:

- Insist that quarterbacks bring the football to the chin with both hands.

- Make sure the quarterbacks do not swing the football away from the body as they move the football to the ear.

- Make sure quarterbacks' follow-through forces them to catch themselves on the ground with their throwing hand.

- Make sure quarterbacks practice the proper mechanics in throwing all passes.

Safety Considerations:

- Proper warm-up should precede drill.

- Helmets should be worn with chinstraps snapped.

- Maintain a minimum distance of five yards between each pair of paired quarterbacks.

Variation:

- Can vary the distance between each pair of paired quarterbacks.

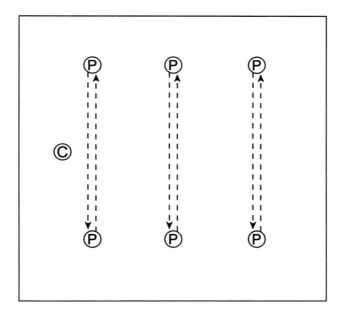

OVER-THE-TOP PASSING*

> **Robert C. "Bobby" Bowden**
> Samford University, West Virginia University, Florida State University
> National Champions: Florida State 1993 and 1999
> National Coach of the Year: Florida State 1979, 1980, 1991 1996, and 1999
> Fellowship of Christian Athletes Grant Teaff Coach of the Year: 2000

Objective: To teach and practice the proper mechanics of passing the football up and over a defensive back in the execution of the take-off route.

Equipment Needed: Footballs

Description:

- Align a center and a quarterback over the football in the middle of the field on the 50-yard line.

- A wide receiver is positioned on the line of scrimmage in the middle of the right outside third of the field. His back foot is placed on the 50-yard line.

- A defensive back is placed with his back to the quarterback and one yard to the inside of the receiver. His front foot is placed on the 50-yard line.

- Other drill participants stand adjacent to their drill area.

- On the cadence and ball snap, the quarterback takes a three-step pass drop as the receiver runs the take-off route with the defensive back in chase.

- The quarterback passes the football 35 yards downfield and over-the-top of the defender and the receiver catches the ball over his outside shoulder.

- The drill continues until all the quarterbacks have thrown a sufficient number of over-the-top passes.

- The drill should be run both left and right.

Coaching Points:

- Always check to see that the quarterbacks are aligned correctly.

- Make sure the center-quarterback exchange is executed properly.

- Make sure all the quarterbacks get plenty of *loft* on each pass.

*Reprinted with permission from *101 Winning Football Drills: From the Legends of the Game* by Jerry Tolley

- Instruct the receivers to sprint full speed staying to the outside of the defenders.
- Insist that all the defenders stay as close to the receivers as possible, thus forcing a perfect pass.
- Make sure all the quarterbacks practice proper mechanics in throwing all passes.

Safety Considerations:
- Proper warm-up should precede the drill.
- The drill area (including sideline areas) should be clear of all foreign articles.
- This drill is not recommended as a contact drill.
- Instruct returning drill participants to stay clear of the drill area.

Variations:
- Can be conducted from either hash mark as well as midfield.
- Can be used as a wide-receiver drill.
- Can be used as a defensive-back drill.
- Can be used as a center-quarterback ball-exchange drill.

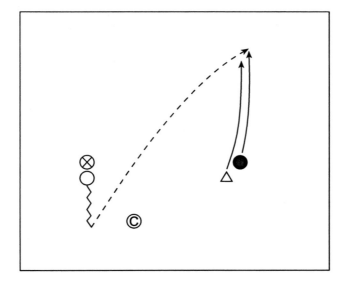

PASS MECHANICS IN WARMING UP

Gary Francis Tranquill
Wittenberg University, Ball State University, Bowling Green State University,
Michigan State University, University of Virginia, Cleveland Browns,
Virginia Polytechnic Institute and State University, West Virginia University,
Ohio State University, United States Naval Academy, University of North Carolina

Objective: To teach and practice the proper mechanics of passing the football with special emphasis on the upper body and arm movement. Can also be used as a warm-up drill.

Equipment Needed: Footballs

Description:

- Align paired quarterbacks in a front-facing position 10 yards apart. Each quarterback pair has a football. Five yards separate each pair of paired quarterbacks.

- At deliberate pace the paired quarterbacks pass the football back and forth from various foot alignments.

- In the first alignment the paired quarterbacks stand flat-footed, with their feet parallel and shoulder-width apart. From this position the football is passed back and forth until all quarterbacks have had a desired number of repetitions.

- Paired quarterbacks now turn sideways to each other and position their feet flat on the ground shoulder-width apart and in a heel-toe relationship. The right foot is forward. Football is passed back and forth as in description three.

- Description four is repeated with quarterbacks placing the left foot forward.

- Now all quarterbacks turn and face in the opposite direction and repeat descriptions four and five.

- The paired quarterbacks once again turn and face each other with their feet positioned in a heel-toe relationship and with the right foot forward. The football is passed back and forth as in other descriptions.

- Description seven is repeated with drill participants placing their left foot forward.

Coaching Points:

- Insist that all passes be thrown from a flat-footed position.

- Make sure all quarterbacks practice the proper mechanics in throwing all passes.

- Emphasize the importance of an exaggerated torso turn when the paired quarterbacks are standing sideways to each other.

Safety Considerations:

- Drill should progress from easy to harder thrown passes.

- Maintain a minimum distance of five yards between each pair of paired quarterbacks.

Variations:

- Can vary the distance between paired quarterbacks.

- Can have quarterbacks aim for an exact spot when passing the footballs to their partners (the head, the numbers, the belt, or the left or right shoulder).

PITCH DRILL

Wallace G. "Wally" English
University of Kentucky, Virginia Polytechnic Institute and State University,
Tulane University, University of Pittsburgh, Brigham Young University,
University of Nebraska, University of Arkansas, Louisville Fire, Miami Dolphins,
Detroit Lions

Objective: To teach and practice the proper fundamentals and techniques of executing the pitch on the option play.

Equipment Needed: Footballs

Description:

- Align two rows of paired quarterbacks five yards apart on two selected yard lines on either side of the field. Each pair of quarterbacks has one football (see diagram).

- On coach's command, the first pair of quarterbacks runs across the field pitching the football back and forth using the desired option pitch technique.

- When the first two drill participants have covered a desired distance, the next two quarterbacks begin their option pitch run across the field.

- When all quarterbacks have crossed the field, the procedure is repeated back to the other sideline.

- Drill continues until all quarterbacks have executed a sufficient number of repetitions.

Coaching Points:

- Make sure that quarterbacks maintain the desired body position throughout the drill.

- When the drill is executed properly, quarterbacks should make four to five pitches as they cross the field.

- Insist that all pitches be executed correctly.

- Instruct all paired quarterbacks to maintain a five-yard separation throughout the drill.

- Insist that the drill be conducted at a realistic speed.

Safety Considerations:

- Proper warm-up should precede drill.

- Drill area (including sideline areas) should be clear of all foreign articles.

- Maintain a minimum distance of 15 yards between each performing pair of paired quarterbacks.

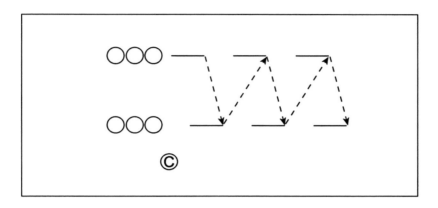

QUARTERBACK SPOT PASSING DRILL

> **Dennis E. Green**
> University of Dayton, University of Iowa, Northwestern University, Stanford University, San Francisco 49ers, Minnesota Vikings, Arizona Cardinals
> National Football League Coach of the Year: Vikings 1992 and 1998

Objective: To teach and practice the proper mechanics of passing the football and reading the open receiver from a five-step pass drop.

Equipment Needed: Footballs

Description:

- Align a quarterback, holding a football, at the left hash mark on a selected line of scrimmage.

- Position three receivers, one on the right hash mark and 12 yards downfield, another on the right hash mark on the line of scrimmage and one more on the left hash mark five yards downfield (see diagram).

- Other quarterbacks stand adjacent to the drill area or may serve as receivers.

- On cadence and snap count, the quarterback takes a five-step pass drop and looks at the receiver positioned 12 yards downfield. If that receiver does not raise his hands, the quarterback looks at the receiver on the line of scrimmage. If that receiver does not raise his hands, the quarterback turns and passes the ball to the receiver on the left hash mark. If either of the preceding receivers had raised his hands, the quarterback would have passed the football to that receiver.

- Drill continues until all quarterbacks have had a sufficient number of repetitions.

- Drill should be run from both the left and right hash marks and from midfield.

Coaching Points:

- Always check to see that quarterbacks are in their proper stances.

- Make sure quarterbacks' pass drops are executed correctly.

- Instruct the receivers not to raise their hands until the quarterback looks in their direction.

- Make sure all quarterbacks practice the proper mechanics in throwing all passes.

Safety Considerations:

- Proper warm-up should precede drill.
- Drill area should be clear of all foreign articles.

Variations:

- Can be used with various quarterback pass drops and receiver alignments.
- Can position receivers to correspond with any selected pass play and quarterback read progression.

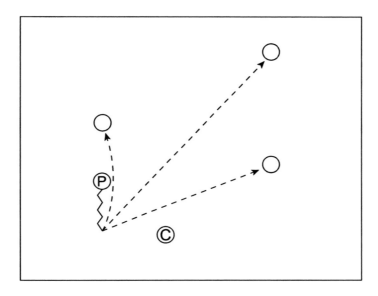

SHORT-STEP CARIOCA*

Steve Spurrier
Georgia Institute of Technology, Tampa Bay Bandits, Duke University,
University of Florida, Washington Redskins, University of South Carolina
National Champions: Florida 1996
National Coach of the Year: Florida 1996

Objective: To teach and practice foot speed, proper head position, viewing the field, and holding the football for a straight drop-back pass.

Equipment Needed: Footballs

Description:

- Align all the quarterbacks five-yards apart on a selected line of scrimmage. Each drill participant holds a football at the post-snap position.

- On the designated quarterback's cadence and snap count, all the quarterbacks pull the balls to and across their chests as each retreats 15 yards using short *carioca* steps (*carioca* stepping is executed at full speed).

- The quarterbacks return to the original line of scrimmage and the procedure is repeated.

- The drill continues until all the quarterbacks have executed a sufficient number of repetitions.

Coaching Points:

- Always check to see that the quarterbacks are in their proper stances.

- Insist that all the quarterbacks pull the football to and across their chests from the post-snap position.

- Make sure the drill is performed at full speed.

- The coach should monitor and record the number of *carioca* steps each quarterback takes in his fifteen-yard pass drop.

- Instruct all the quarterbacks to cock their heads as far to the left as possible, focusing on an object high and far away as they execute their pass drops (right-handed quarterback).

*Reprinted with permission from 101 Winning Football Drills: From the Legends of the Game by Jerry Tolley

Safety Considerations:

- Proper warm-up should precede the drill.

- The drill area should be clear of all foreign articles.

- Instruct all personnel as to the correct techniques in performing the *carioca* stepping.

- Maintain a minimum distance of five yards between performing drill participants.

Variations:

- Can be used with various quarterback drops.

- Can incorporate a center and use as a center-quarterback ball-exchange drill.

QUICK RELEASE DRILL

Jeffrey L. "Jeff" Petrucci
California University of Pennsylvania

Objective: To teach and practice the proper mechanics of passing and releasing the football at the proper time.

Equipment Needed: Four cones, footballs, and a fence

Description:

- Align two cones five yards apart on a designated line. A second pair of cones is placed four yards directly behind the first pair of cones (see diagram).

- If possible, the drill area should be set up in front of a fence or net that acts as a backstop.

- A quarterback, holding a football, lines up 10 yards in front of the first two cones (see diagram).

- Position a defensive back between the front two cones facing the quarterback.

- A receiver is placed four yards behind the defensive back.

- Other drill participants line up adjacent to drill area.

- On quarterback's command, the receiver moves between the back two cones in an attempt to get open. The defensive back is instructed always to look forward reading the quarterback.

- When ready, the quarterback passes the football with a quick release to the receiver, as the defensive back tries to intercept or deflect the pass.

- Drill continues until all quarterbacks have thrown a sufficient number of quick release passes.

Coaching Points:

- Emphasis should be placed on the quarterbacks' quick release.

- Instruct the quarterbacks to look the defensive back *off* the pass.

- Make sure all quarterbacks practice the proper mechanics in throwing all passes.

Safety Considerations:

- Proper warm-up should precede drill.

- A distance of four yards should always be maintained between the receiver and the defensive back.

- It is imperative that the back two cones be placed no closer than seven yards from the fence or net area.

Variations:

- The quarterback can vary his distance from the defensive back.

- Can be used as defensive back and linebacker drill.

- Can be used as a tight end and wide receiver drill.

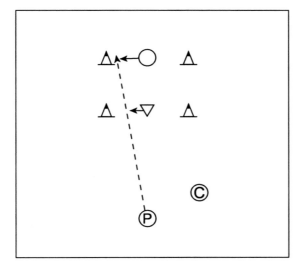

STEP-AND-THROW DRILL*

R. LaVell Edwards
Brigham Young University
National Champions: 1984
National Coach of the Year: 1984
College Football Hall of Fame: 2004
AFCA President: 1987
Amos Alonzo Stagg Award: 2003

Objective: To teach and practice taking the proper step angle in passing the football to a particular receiver. Incorporated are skills of setting-up, reading, quickness, and agility.

Equipment Needed: Footballs

Description:

- Align a quarterback and a center over the football at the midpoint of a selected line of scrimmage.

- Place four receivers at ending positions of a designated pass pattern (see diagram).

- Other quarterbacks stand adjacent to the drill area or serve as receivers.

- On the cadence and ball snap, the quarterback executes his pass drop according to the play called and follows his proper read progression against a designated (simulated) coverage.

- The coach who is positioned behind the quarterback signals to one of the four receivers to raise his hand.

- As the designated receiver raises his hand, the quarterback passes him the football.

- The drill continues until all the quarterbacks have had a sufficient number of repetitions.

- The drill should be run from both the left and right hash marks as well as from midfield.

Coaching Points:

- Always check to see that the quarterbacks are in their proper stances.

- Make sure the center-quarterback exchange is executed correctly.

---

*Reprinted with permission from *101 Winning Football Drills: From the Legends of the Game* by Jerry Tolley

- Instruct the quarterbacks to follow their read progression with each pass thrown.
- Insist that all the quarterbacks continue to shuffle their feet as they complete their read progression.
- Make sure all the quarterbacks take the proper stepping angle when throwing to a particular receiver.
- Make sure all the quarterbacks practice the proper mechanics in throwing all passes.

Safety Considerations:

- Proper warm-up should precede the drill.
- The drill area should be clear of all foreign articles.

Variations:

- Can be used with various quarterback-pass drops and receiver alignments.
- Can incorporate a hot pass when the quarterback has to alter his pass drop.

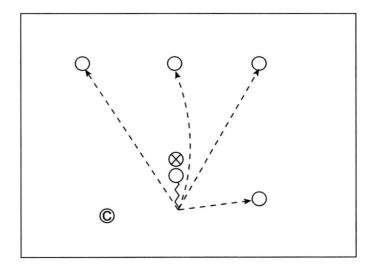

SCAN DRILL

Darryl D. Rogers
Fresno City College, California State University-Hayward, Fresno State University, San Jose State University, Michigan State University, Arizona State University, Detroit Lions, Winnipeg Blue Bombers

Objective: To teach and practice proper mechanics of passing the football including taking the correct pass drop steps and scanning the secondary.

Equipment Needed: Footballs

Description:

- Align a quarterback and a center over the football at the midpoint of a selected line of scrimmage.

- Place three receivers 15 yards apart on a yard line 10 yards downfield. The middle receiver lines head up the center (see diagram).

- Other quarterbacks line up adjacent to drill area or may serve as receivers.

- The coach stands 15 yards behind the quarterback.

- On cadence and ball snap, the quarterback executes his designated pass drop as the coach signals one of the three receivers to raise his hand.

- When the designated receiver raises his hand, the quarterback passes him the football.

- After the first quarterback takes four repetitions, the next quarterback takes his turn, and so on.

- Drill continues until all quarterbacks have had a sufficient number of repetitions.

- Drill should be run from both the left and right hash marks as well as from midfield.

Coaching Points:

- Always check to see that quarterbacks are in their proper stances.

- Make sure the center-quarterback ball exchange is executed properly.

- Check to see that all quarterbacks take their proper pass drop steps.

- Instruct the quarterbacks to scan the entire field focusing on all receivers.

- The coach should vary the tempo of his signals to require the quarterbacks to throw hot passes in the middle of their pass drops.

- Make sure all quarterbacks practice the proper mechanics in throwing all passes.

Safety Considerations:

- Proper warm-up should precede drill.

- Drill area should be clear of all foreign articles.

Variations:

- Can be used with various quarterback pass drops and receiver alignments.

- Can be used with only one receiver to concentrate on quarterback's pass drops.

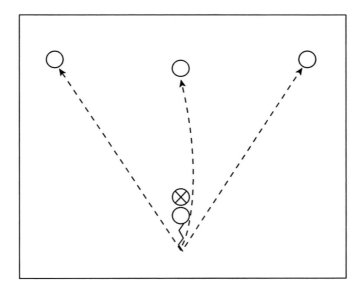

BALL HANDLING DRILL

Joseph "Joe" Restic
Brown University, Colgate University, Hamilton Tiger-Cats, Harvard University

Objective: To teach and practice the proper mechanics of handling and faking the football in the execution of various offensive play actions passes.

Equipment Needed: Line-spacing strip and football

Description:

- Place a line spacing strip on a selected line of scrimmage.
- Align a skeleton offense (quarterback, running backs, and receivers) on the selected line of scrimmage relative to the play to be run.
- Alternating skeleton offenses stand adjacent to the drill area.
- The quarterback is positioned in a pre-snap alignment with a football in each hand. He calls out the formation and the play action play to be executed.
- On his cadence and snap count, the quarterback hands a football to the first back in the play and then hands the other one to the second back.
- Or the quarterback can hand the football to the first or second back and then pass the football to the designated receiver (see diagram).
- Drill continues with quarterback calling a variety of play-action passes from various offensive alignments.

Coaching Points:

- Always check to see that all personnel are aligned correctly and are in their proper stances.
- Make sure quarterbacks execute all handoffs, fakes, and passes properly.
- Stress the importance of the single-hand handoff.
- After the first handoff is executed, instruct the quarterback to secure the second football with both hands.
- Make sure all quarterbacks practice the proper mechanics in throwing all passes.

Safety Considerations:

- Proper warm-up should precede drill.

- Drill area should be cleared of all foreign articles.

- Make sure helmets are worn and chinstraps are snapped.

Variations:

- Can be used as a running back and receiving drill.

- Can be used with various off-tackle and *waggle*-action pass plays.

- Can be used with dive or trap action plays.

- Can be used with screen and draw action plays.

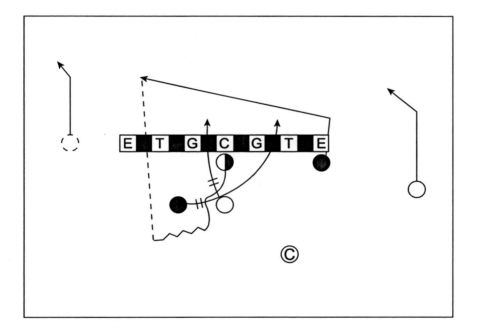

WAVE DRILL*

Bob Ford
Albright College, Springfield College, St. Lawrence University, University at Albany
AFCA President: 2000

Objective: To teach and practice the skills of moving forward and laterally in avoiding a pass rush while keeping the football at the ready-to-pass position.

Equipment Needed: Footballs

Description:

- Align two rows of quarterbacks 15-yards apart and facing one another on two selected lines of scrimmage. Five yards should separate the quarterbacks on the same line of scrimmage (see diagram).

- The coach is positioned in the middle of the drill area.

- On a designated quarterback's cadence and snap count, all the quarterbacks on his line of scrimmage execute a five-step pass drop.

- When this row of quarterbacks takes their fifth drop step, the coach waves for them to move either to their left or to their right.

- After the row of quarterbacks has moved to either the left or the right, the coach now signals the quarterbacks to pass the football to the front-facing quarterbacks in the opposite row by bringing his hand forward and to the ground.

- The drill continues until the alternating rows of quarterbacks have had a sufficient number of repetitions moving both to the left and the right.

Coaching Points:

- Always check to see that the quarterbacks are in their proper stance.

- Make sure that the quarterbacks' five-step drops are executed correctly.

- Insist that the quarterbacks always practice the proper mechanics in throwing all passes.

- Insist that the quarterbacks always keep their feet, shoulders, and throwing arm in the *ready-to-pass* position throughout the drill.

---

*Reprinted with permission from *101 Winning Football Drills: From the Legends of the Game* by Jerry Tolley

- Instruct the quarterbacks to always have both hands on the football and to be ready to move either to the left or the right, and to throw the football on the coach's signal.

Safety Considerations:

- Proper warm-up should precede the drill.

- The drill area should be clear of all foreign articles.

- The coach should make sure he is never in the line of fire of the quarterbacks' passes.

Variations:

- Can be used with a variety of pass drops, sprint outs, and rollouts.

- The coach can wave the quarterback from side to side before signaling for the passes to be thrown.

- The coach can signal the quarterback to pass the football after the quarterbacks completes their initial five-step drop.

- The coach can signal the quarterbacks to move forward before passing the football.

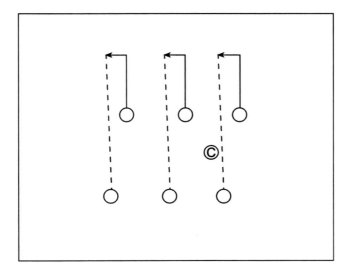

ELWAY'S WAY

John Albert "Jack" Elway (Deceased)
Grays Harbor College, University of Montana, Washington State University,
California State University-Northridge, San Jose State University, Stanford University,
Frankfurt Galaxy, Denver Broncos

Objective: To teach and practice the proper mechanics of passing the football. Can also be used as a warm-up drill.

Equipment Needed: Footballs

Description:

- Align paired quarterbacks in a front-facing position 10 yards apart with a football. Five yards should separate each pair of paired quarterbacks.
- On coach's instructions, all quarterbacks kneel on the right knee.
- From this position, quarterbacks throw twenty-five passes
- Description three is repeated with all quarterbacks kneeling on the left knee.

Coaching Points:

- Make sure all quarterbacks *grip* the football properly.
- Insist that all quarterbacks exaggerate their throwing motion by letting their wrists turn over with each pass thrown.
- Emphasis should be placed on the throwing motion, the release, and the follow-through as well as the accuracy of the pass.
- Make sure all quarterbacks practice the proper mechanics in throwing all passes.

Safety Considerations:

- Maintain a minimum distance of five yards between each pair of paired drill participants.
- Drill should progress from easy to harder thrown passes.

Variations:

- Can vary the distance between paired drill participants.
- Drill can progress from the knees to standing one-step, three-step, and five-step pass drops.

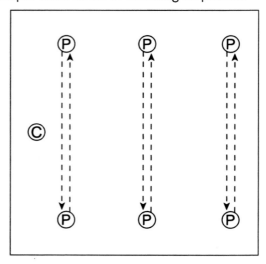

5

Center-Quarterback Ball Exchange Drills

CENTER-QUARTERBACK EXCHANGE

Gregg Brandon
Weber State University, University of Wyoming, Utah State University,
Northwestern University, University of Colorado, Bowling Green State University

Objective: To teach and practice the proper fundamentals and techniques in the execution of the center-quarterback exchange. Incorporated are the various first steps and paths of the center and quarterback in the execution of designated plays.

Equipment Needed: Footballs

Description:

- Align the desired number of center-quarterback pairs five yards apart on a selected line of scrimmage.

- The coach is positioned in front of the paired centers and quarterbacks and calls out the play to be run (see diagram).

- Each quarterback in turn is designated the signal caller and calls out the cadence and snap count.

- On designated quarterback's cadence, all centers execute the center snap and take the first three steps of the play designated by the coach.

- Each quarterback receives the snap from the center and takes the steps designated by the play.

- Drill continues until all centers and quarterbacks have had a sufficient number of repetitions in executing the first steps of various plays called by the coach.

Coaching Points:

- Always check to see that all personnel are aligned correctly and are in their proper stances.

- Instruct the centers to take the football with the laces up. (When this is done the football will turn *naturally* into the quarterbacks' top hand.)

- As the centers snap the football, insist that they take the proper first three steps of the called play.

- In receiving the snap, the quarterback's hands should be *together* with the bottom hand's thumb set in the *groove* of the top hand's thumb. The index finger of the top hand should run through the middle of the center's *butt*. The bottom hand must push all the pressure of both hands to *ride* the center's *butt* as the snap is being executed.

- Instruct the quarterbacks that the fingers should be kept wide at all times until the snap is received.
- As the football is snapped, make sure the quarterbacks *ride* the bottom hand and *close* on the football and to take their first steps as designated by the play.
- Instruct the quarterbacks to always secure (*seed*) the football in their stomachs.

Safety Considerations:

- Proper warm-up should precede drill.
- Always maintain a five-yard separation between each center-quarterback pair.
- Drill area should be clear of all foreign articles.

Variations:

- Can be used with a defender positioned over each center in various defensive alignments. At the discretion of the coach, the defenders can hold a hand shield.
- Can be used with various running back or one-man pass route actions.
- Can be used in executing the snap from the shotgun formation.

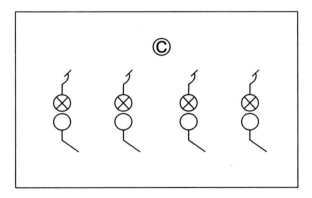

CENTER-QUARTERBACK EXCHANGE

Timothy "Tim" Murphy
Lafayette College, Boston University, University of Maine, University of Cincinnati, Harvard University

Objective: To teach and practice the proper fundamentals and techniques in the execution of the center-quarterback ball exchange. Incorporated is the development of ball *security* for the center, quarterback, and running back.

Equipment Needed: Three blocking shields and footballs

Description:

- Align three centers five yards apart on a selected line of scrimmage.

- A defender, holding a blocking shield, is positioned over each center.

- Align a quarterback and a running back in their normal alignment behind each center. The running back should be seven yards behind the quarterback (see diagram).

- Other drill participants stand adjacent to their drill area.

- The coach stands behind the offense.

- On designated quarterback's play call, cadence, and snap count, the three centers execute the *perfect* snap while exploding out of their stance and blocking the defenders.

- The defenders react to the centers' block and steps forward resisting the block at three-quarter speed.

- The three quarterbacks execute the appropriate *footwork* for the play called and hand the football off to the tailbacks.

- The running back executes the appropriate footwork for the play called and runs the proper play path five yards beyond the line of scrimmage.

- Drill continues until all drill participants have had a sufficient number of repetitions in running selected plays both left and right.

Coaching Points:

- Always check to see that all drill participants are aligned correctly and are in their proper stances.

- Emphasize the importance of executing the *perfect* center-quarterback exchange with every ball snap.

- Insist that the centers *explode* out of their stance and block the defenders as they snap the football.

- Instruct the centers to hold the football with the laces up, and when snapping the football to rotate the football with a one-quarter turn so that the laces will fit *naturally* in the quarterbacks' fingertips.

- Instruct the quarterbacks to keep upward pressure on the centers' butt until the football is *secure* in their hands.

- Emphasize the importance of *securing* the football by all drill participants on every play.

- Insist that the running backs sprint five yards past the line of scrimmage on all plays.

Safety Considerations:

- Proper warm-up should precede drill.

- The drill area should be clear of all foreign articles.

- For safety purposes, the drill should be run at slightly less than full speed.

- Always check to see that all center, quarterback, and running back groups maintain a five-yard separation.

- Stress the importance of all drill participants' concentrating on the play call to avoid unnecessary collisions.

Variations:

- Can be used with the defender aligned *head-up* or in a left or right *shade* alignment on the center.

- Can be used in the execution of various pass drop and center-blocking techniques.

- Can be used with a variety of running plays to change the footwork for quarterbacks and running backs, and blocking techniques for centers.

- Can be used with a shotgun formation for the execution of shotgun center snaps for both running and passing plays.

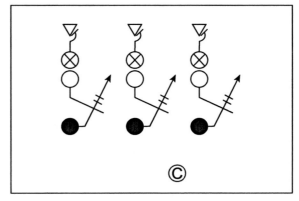

CENTER-QUARTERBACK EXCHANGE AND BLOCKING

Thomas W. "Tom" Jackson
Millersville University, State University of New York College at Cortland,
University of Connecticut

Objective: To teach and practice the proper fundamentals and techniques in the execution of the center-quarterback ball exchange. Incorporated are various blocking assignments.

Equipment Needed: Large blocking dummy, hand shield, and football

Description:

- Align a center and a quarterback in their normal positions on a selected line of scrimmage. The quarterback holds a football.

- Position a nose guard and a backside linebacker in their normal defensive positions. The nose guard holds a dummy and the linebacker holds a hand shield (see diagram).

- Alternating drill participants stand adjacent to the drill area.

- At deliberate pace the quarterback places the football in the center's *crotch*. The center reaches back and takes the football. The procedure is repeated until both the quarterback and center have a feel for the exchange position.

- Now on quarterback's cadence, the center snaps the football and executes various blocking assignments as the defenders react and stunt.

- Drill continues until all center-quarterback exchange combinations have had a sufficient number of repetitions.

- Drill should be run with backside linebacker positioned both left and right of the center.

Coaching Points:

- Always check to see that all personnel are aligned correctly and are in their proper stances.

- Make sure center-quarterback ball exchange is executed correctly.

- Instruct centers always to step to and work for play side leverage.

- Make sure the quarterbacks have a secure hold on the football before they move away from the center.

- Emphasis should be more on the center-quarterback ball exchange than on blocking.

- Insist that the drill be conducted at full speed.

Safety Considerations:

- Proper warm-up should precede drill.

- Instruct the centers to keep their heads up at all times.

- Instruct the quarterbacks to keep their hands in to accept the snap correctly.

Variation:

- Can be used with defenders in various alignments.

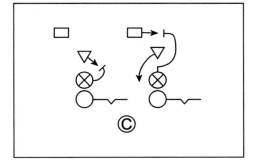

ON THE LINE

M. Wayne Grubb
Samford University, University of North Alabama, Birmingham Americans
National Champions: Samford 1971 (Vacated)

Objective: To teach and practice the proper fundamentals and techniques in the execution of the center-quarterback ball exchange.

Equipment Needed: Large blocking dummies and footballs

Description:

- Align a desired number of center-quarterback pairs four yards apart on a selected line of scrimmage.
- A defender holding a dummy is positioned over each center.
- A quarterback is designated to select a play and to call cadence.
- On cadence the centers snap the footballs and all quarterbacks and centers execute the steps and techniques of the play called.
- Drill continues until rotating quarterbacks have had a sufficient number of snap exchanges with each center.

Coaching Points:

- Always check to see that all personnel are in their proper stances.
- Instruct the centers to *sweep* the football back with their elbows locked as they step to execute their blocks.
- Instruct all quarterbacks to apply pressure upward so the centers can get the feel for the snap.
- Make sure that the quarterbacks' hands *ride* forward as the centers snap the football and drive out of their stances.
- Emphasis should be more on the center-quarterback snap exchange than on blocking.
- Insist that the drill be conducted at full speed.

Safety Considerations:

- Proper warm-up should precede drill.

- Instruct the quarterbacks always to open their hands and extend their fingers as they receive the snap.

- Remind the centers always to keep their heads up.

- Always maintain a minimum distance of four yards between each pair of paired centers and quarterbacks.

Variation:

- Can be used as a form or live blocking drill.

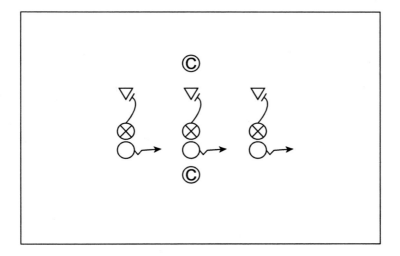

SNAPPING DRILL

Ray Alborn
Rice University, Lamar University, Houston Gamblers

Objective: To teach and practice the proper fundamentals and techniques in the execution of the center-quarterback ball exchange.

Equipment Needed: Three large blocking dummies and footballs

Description:

- Align a center and a quarterback in their normal positions over the football on a selected line of scrimmage.

- Lay a large blocking dummy perpendicular to the line of scrimmage at the nose guard and defensive end positions (see diagram).

- Other drill participants stand adjacent to the drill area.

- On quarterback's cadence the center snaps the football and both the quarterback and center execute the steps and techniques of a previously selected play. (Plays selected should include those that require the center to execute drive blocks, reach blocks, pass blocks, and pulling techniques).

- Drill continues until rotating quarterbacks have had a sufficient number of repetitions of selected play with each center.

Coaching Points:

- Always check to see that all personnel are in their proper stances.

- Make sure that the center-quarterback ball exchange is executed properly.

- Make sure all centers take their correct steps and use the proper techniques in the execution of the different blocks.

- Instruct the quarterbacks to use the audible system.

- Emphasis should be more on the center-quarterback exchange than on blocking assignments.

- Insist that the drill be conducted at full speed.

Safety Considerations:

- Proper warm-up should precede drill.

- Drill area should be clear of all foreign articles.

Variation:

- Can be used with all plays and all center blocking schemes.

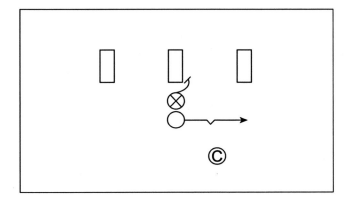

6

Tight End Drills

ESCAPE DRILL

Albert Michael "Al" Groh
United States Military Academy, University of North Carolina,
United States Air Force Academy, Texas Tech University, University of South Carolina,
Wake Forest University, New England Patriots, Cleveland Browns, New York Giants,
Atlanta Falcons, New York Jets, University of Virginia

Objective: To teach and practice the proper fundamentals and techniques in executing the inside and outside line releases.

Equipment Needed: One large blocking dummy and one hand shield

Description:

- Position a tight end in his stance on a selected line of scrimmage.

- A defensive end holding a hand shield is positioned over the outside shoulder of the tight end.

- Other tight ends stand adjacent to drill area.

- Lay a large dummy in the neutral zone at the tackle position (see diagram).

- On coach's cadence, the tight end releases off the line of scrimmage executing either a *swim* or *lower shoulder drive* technique.

- The defender *jams* the tight end in an attempt to prevent his release.

- Drill continues until all tight ends have had a sufficient number of inside and outside release repetitions using both the *swim* and *low shoulder drive* techniques.

- Drill should be conducted from both left and right formations.

Coaching Points:

- Always check to see that tight ends are in their proper stances.

- In executing the *swim* technique, instruct tight ends to fake in the opposite direction of the release. They then *jam* the defender's release side elbow toward his hip and execute the *swim* technique with the opposite arm over the top of the defender.

- In executing the *low shoulder drive* technique, the tight ends are instructed to fake in the opposite direction of the release. They then drive their release side shoulders under the defenders.

Safety Considerations:

- Proper warm-up should precede drill.

- The coach should monitor closely the intensity of the drill.

- Instruct the shield holder not to *jam* the tight end in the head area.

- Instruct the tight ends as to the proper fundamentals and techniques in executing the various releases.

Variation:

- Can be used with the defender positioned head up and inside and outside the tight end.

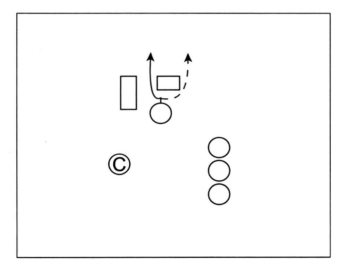

HASH*

Joseph Dennis "Joe" Taylor
Eastern Illinois University, Howard University, Virginia Union University,
Hampton University
National Black College Champions: Hampton 1994 and 1997
National Black College Coach of the Year: Hampton 1994 and 1997
AFCA President: 2001

Objective: To teach and practice the proper techniques in getting open in the underneath hash area.

Equipment Needed: Three large blocking dummies and footballs

Description:

- Align rows of tight ends perpendicular to and five-yards inside and outside the right hash mark on a selected line of scrimmage.

- Position-held dummies 12-yards downfield on the hash mark and five yards to the left and right of the hash marks.

- A quarterback holding a football is positioned on the line of scrimmage between the two lines of receivers.

- On the quarterback's cadence and snap count, the designated tight end releases from the line and works the space between the two dummies on his side of the hash marks. If the quarterback does not pass him the football between the first two dummies, the tight end works for a position between the other pair of dummies and away from pressure.

- The quarterback is instructed to execute a designated pass drop and pass the football to the tight end between either pair of held dummies or away from pressure.

- After catching the pass, the tight end turns and sprints upfield. He then returns to the opposite receiving line.

- The drill continues until all the tight ends have had a sufficient number of repetitions.

- The drill should be conducted from both the left and right hash marks and from various field positions.

*Reprinted with permission from *101 Winning Football Drills: From the Legends of the Game* by Jerry Tolley

Coaching Points:

- Always check to see that the tight ends are aligned correctly and are in their proper stances.

- Instruct the tight ends to execute their release techniques (rip or swim) correctly.

- Insist that all the tight ends maintain a good *football position* as they work to get open between the dummies. (Instruct tight ends to move laterally without drifting in depth.)

- Insist that the drill be conducted at full speed.

Safety Considerations:

- Proper warm-up should precede the drill.

- The drill area should be clear of all foreign articles.

- Helmets should be worn with chinstraps snapped.

Variations:

- Can be used with a defender holding a hand shield over the tight end to prevent his release off the line.

- Can be used as a wide-receiver drill.

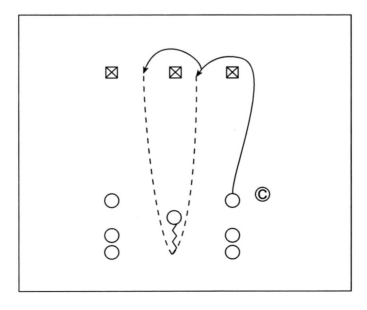

TEACHING THE DRIVE BLOCK

George Small
Langston University, Savannah State University, University of Tulsa,
Florida A&M University, Grambling State University; Kentucky State University,
Youngstown State University, Hampton University, North Carolina A&T State University

Objective: To teach and practice the proper fundments and techniques in the execution of the drive block on a defensive end aligned in an outside *shade* position. Special attention is paid to obtaining the correct 45-degree blocking angle.

Equipment Needed: Board (6" x 2" x 6')

Description:

- Align a tight end in his normal stance on a selected line of scrimmage.

- Position a defensive end, holding a hand shield, in an outside shade alignment over the tight end.

- Other drill participants stand adjacent to the drill area.

- Place the blocking board adjacent to the outside foot of the tight end and at a 45-degree angle to the defensive end (see diagram).

- The coach is positioned behind the tight end.

- On coach's cadence and snap count, the tight end takes a 45-degree angle step toward the defensive end with his outside foot and *straddles* the board.

- Description six is repeated at the discretion of the coach.

- Drill continues by repeating description six with the tight end now executing a drive block on the defensive end—who is reaction to the tight end's movement.

- Drill continues until all tight ends have had a sufficient number of repetitions.

- Drill should be conducted from both left and right alignments.

Coaching Points:

- Always check to see that the tight ends are aligned correctly and are in their proper stances.

- Instruct the tight ends to always take their first step toward the defensive end with the outside foot *straddling* the board. Doing so will ensure that the hips will be opened and the shoulders will be aligned at the proper 45-degree blocking angle to the defensive end.

- Make sure that the tight ends' second step (with the inside foot) splits the crotch of the defensive end.

- Insist that the tight ends contact the defensive end with the head up, shoulders *squared* to the defender, and with the feet shoulder-width apart and driving.

- Make sure all tight ends use the proper fundamentals and techniques in the execution of the drive block.

Safety Considerations:

- Proper warm-up should precede drill.

- The drill area should be clear of all foreign articles.

- The drill should progress from walk-through to full speed.

- The coach should monitor closely the intensity of the drill.

- The board should be beveled and checked for splinters daily.

- Instruct the tight ends as to the proper fundamentals and techniques of the drive block.

Variations:

- Can be used without the blocking board.

- Can be used to teach other tight end blocks, especially combination zone blocking schemes with the offensive tackles.

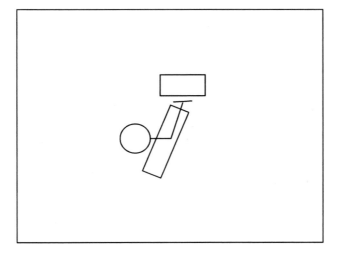

TIGHT END BLOCKING*

James M. "Jim" Christopherson
Concordia College (Moorhead)
National Champions: 1978 and 1981
National Coach of the Year: 1981

Objective: To teach and practice the proper fundamentals and techniques in blocking the gap, reach, and arch blocks.

Equipment Needed: None

Description:

- Align a tight end in his stance on a selected line of scrimmage.
- Position a defensive end or a linebacker in his normal alignment over the tight end.
- Other drill participants will stand adjacent to the drill area.
- On the quarterback's (coach's) cadence and snap count, the tight end executes the designated blocking technique that was called in the huddle (gap, reach, or arch). (See the following diagrams.)
- The drill continues until all the tight ends have had a sufficient number of repetitions executing the gap, reach, and arch blocks.
- The drill should be conducted from both left and right formations.

Coaching Points:

- Always check to see that the tight ends are aligned correctly and are in their proper stance.
- Instruct the tight ends on the proper techniques in executing the gap, reach, and arch blocks. This is especially true in regard to footwork.
- In the execution of the gap and reach blocks, emphasis should be placed on making contact at the correct *blocking point* on the defender.
- In executing the reach block, the tight ends should be instructed to *jolt* the defensive end before maneuvering their body into an outside blocking position.
- The emphasis of drill should be on repetition and not contact.

---

*Reprinted with permission from *101 Winning Football Drills: From the Legends of the Game* by Jerry Tolley

Safety Considerations:

- Proper warm-up should precede the drill.
- The drill should progress from formwork to live work.
- Helmets should be worn and chinstraps snapped.
- The drill area should be clear of all foreign articles.

Variation:

- Can be used as a defensive-end, linebacker, and defensive-back drill.

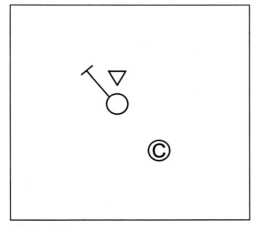

Diagram A

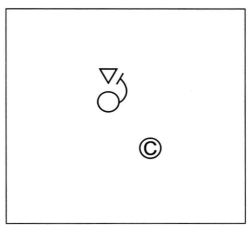

Diagram B

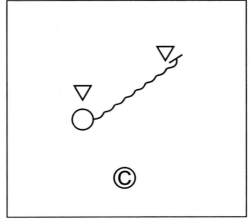

Diagram C

INSIDE RELEASE DRILL

Pat Collins
University of Louisiana-Monroe, Arkansas State University, Miami Tribe,
Northeast Louisiana University, Louisiana Tech University
National Champions: Louisiana Tech 1987
National Coach of the Year: Louisiana Tech 1987

Objective: To teach and practice the proper fundamentals and techniques of executing an inside line release.

Equipment Needed: A large blocking dummy, two cones, and footballs

Description:

- Lay a large blocking dummy in the neutral zone at the offensive tackle position on a selected line of scrimmage. Place two cones downfield relative to the positions of the pass drop of two inside linebackers (see diagram).

- Position a tight end in his stance in his normal position. Other tight ends stand behind the first drill performer.

- A defensive end is aligned over the tight end and is instructed to prevent his release.

- The quarterback (coach), holding a football, is positioned in his normal alignment in relationship to the tight end.

- On quarterback's (coach's) cadence and snap count, the tight end executes his inside release and runs his predetermined pass route and catches the pass thrown by the quarterback and turns and sprints upfield (see diagram).

- Drill continues until all tight ends have had a sufficient number of repetitions.

- Drill should be conducted both left and right and from various field positions.

Coaching Points:

- Always check to see that tight ends are aligned correctly and are in their proper stances.

- In executing the inside release, instruct tight ends to take a *short jab* step at a 45-degree angle to the inside with the inside foot. They should then drive upfield off the inside foot and escape the defensive end by executing a forearm blow to the inside shoulder of the defensive end.

- Instruct the tight ends not to use crossover steps.
- Insist that all tight ends execute their predetermined pass routes correctly and at full speed.

Safety Considerations:

- Proper warm-up should precede drill.
- Drill area should be clear of all foreign articles.
- The coach should monitor closely the intensity of the drill.
- Instruct the defensive end not to be overly aggressive in preventing the tight end's release.
- Instruct the tight ends as to the proper fundamentals and techniques in executing the inside release.

Variations:

- Can be used as an outside release drill.
- Can be used as a slot back drill.
- Can incorporate linebackers.
- Can be used as a linebacker and defensive end drill.

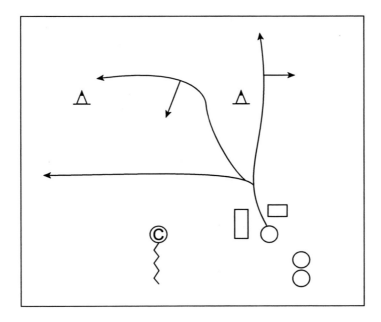

OPEN-UP DRILL

Daniel Leon Kratzer
Lindenwood University, Hasting College, Missouri Valley College,
Miami University (Ohio), Ohio Northern University, Indiana University,
San Francisco 49ers, Kent State University

Objective: To teach and practice the proper fundamentals and techniques of catching a pass thrown behind a tight end. Incorporated are skills related to reaction, changing direction, and body control.

Equipment Needed: Two large blocking dummies and footballs

Description:

- Position a quarterback, holding a football, at the midpoint of a selected line of scrimmage.

- Lay two large blocking dummies five yards apart, 25 yards downfield, and in front of the quarterback (see diagram).

- Position a row of tight ends 20 yards downfield and 10 yards to the right of the dummy area.

- On quarterback's command, the first tight end runs across the field. When he approaches the plane of the second dummy, the quarterback releases a pass that is thrown slightly behind the tight end. The tight end adjusts to the football, makes the catch, tucks the football away, and sprints up field between the two dummies.

- Drill continues until all tight ends have had a sufficient number of repetitions.

- Drill should be conducted both left and right.

Coaching Points:

- Make sure tight ends use the correct running form as they run across the field.

- In turning to catch the football when thrown behind the tight end (when running from right to left), instruct tight ends to plant the upfield foot (right foot) and open up the hips by pivoting on the right foot and turning the left hand and left leg back toward the football. Now it is important for the tight ends to follow through by having the right hand trail the left hand catching the football with both hands, tucking it away, and turning and sprinting upfield.

- Insist that tight ends sprint between the dummies after the catch is made.

Safety Considerations:

- Proper warm-up should precede drill.

- Drill area should be clear of all foreign articles.

- Helmets should be worn with chinstraps snapped.

Variations:

- Can be used with tight end running a variety of pass routes.

- Can be used as a wide receiver drill.

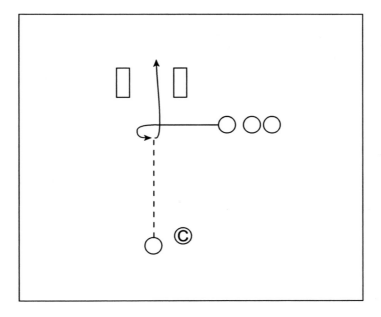

SPEED RELEASE*

Roger N. Harring
University of Wisconsin-La Crosse
National Champions: 1985, 1992, and 1995
National Coach of the Year: 1992 and 1995

Objective: To teach the proper use of the hands in executing the speed release. Incorporated are skills related to quickness and concentration.

Equipment Needed: Large plastic wiffleball bat

Description:

- Align a row of tight ends on a selected line of scrimmage. Approximately one yard separates the tight ends (see diagram).

- The coach, holding a wiffleball bat, positions himself in front of the row of tight ends.

- On the coach's command, all the tight ends assume the quarter-eagle football position while *buzzing* their feet.

- The coach now walks directly toward the row of tight ends pointing the wiffleball bat at the outside numbers of each drill participant. (The coach is simulating a defensive end's attempt to grab and hold up the tight end's release.)

- As the coach walks toward each tight end in sequence, the tight ends execute a quick slap with the outside hand, knocking the wiffleball bat out of the way. Simultaneously, the tight ends turn their hips and shoulders as each executes a *carioca* step to clear their hips past the coach (defender).

- After the coach passes the last tight end in the row, the drill is repeated with the tight ends now facing the opposite direction.

- The drill continues until all the tight ends have had a sufficient number of repetitions using both the left and right hand slaps.

Coaching Points:

- Always check to see that the tight ends are in the quarter-eagle position and are *buzzing* their feet.

- Instruct all the tight ends to use the proper hand-slap technique.

*Reprinted with permission from *101 Winning Football Drills: From the Legends of the Game* by Jerry Tolley

- Emphasize the importance of the tight ends working to clear their hips while simultaneously delivering the hand slap.

Safety Considerations:

- Proper warm-up should precede the drill.
- Helmets should be worn with chinstraps snapped.
- The wiffleball bat should be checked periodically for cracks and rough spots.

Variations:

- Can be used with the offensive ends coming out of a three-point stance.
- Can be used as a wide-receiver drill in teaching the release against a *jam* corner.
- Can incorporate a quarterback and execute a designated pass route after the release.

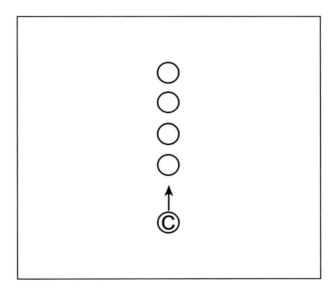

REACTION DRILL

Michael "Mike" Price
University of Missouri, University of Puget Sound, Weber State University,
Washington State University, University of Texas-El Paso,
National Coach of the Year: Washington State 1997

Objective: To teach and practice the proper fundamentals and techniques of catching the football with special emphasis on concentration.

Equipment Needed: Football

Description:

- Align a passer (coach) with a football on a selected line of scrimmage.

- Position a tight end with his back to the passer 10 yards downfield. Other tight ends line up behind the first tight end.

- On passer's (coach's) command, the first tight end *buzzes* his feet. On passer's second command, the tight end snaps his head and shoulders around and catches the football that the passer has thrown. The passer (coach) can throw the pass at any time before or after giving the second command.

- After making the catch, the tight end tucks the football away and sprints to the coach and hands him the football.

- Drill continues until all tight ends have had a sufficient number of repetitions catching the football after turning both to the left and right.

Coaching Points:

- Insist that all tight ends actively *buzz* their feet.

- Instruct all tight ends to turn their heads first and then the rest of their bodies as they turn and face the passer.

- Insist that the tight ends catch the football in their hands.

- Make sure that all tight ends tuck the football away before they sprint to the passer.

Safety Considerations:

- Proper warm-up should precede drill.
- Helmets should be worn with chinstraps snapped.
- Instruct alternating drill participants always to remain alert.

Variations:

- Can be used with tight ends positioned on their knees and facing the passer.
- Can be used with the passer aligned at varying distances from the tight ends.
- Can be used with passer throwing the football at varying velocities and trajectories.
- Can be used for all pass-receiving positions.

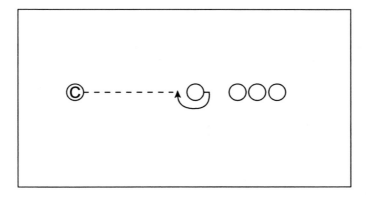

READ DOWN DRILL

Robert D. Curtis
Franklin and Marshall College, Bucknell University, Shippensburg University

Objectives: To teach and practice the proper fundamentals and techniques of reading the defense and executing the *down* block.

Equipment Needed: One large blocking dummy and two hand shields

Description:

- Review the fundamentals and techniques of executing the *down* block on the blackboard in a group meeting.

- Align an offensive tackle and a tight end in their normal positions on a selected line of scrimmage.

- Position a defensive end, a tackle, and an onside linebacker in their normal alignments over the offense. (The tackle holds a blocking dummy and the end and linebacker hold hand shields.)

- Other tight ends stand adjacent to drill area.

- The coach walks through and explains the various rules, fundamentals, and techniques of the *down* block with the offensive tackle and tight ends (see diagram).

- On coach's cadence and snap count, the tackle and tight end execute their various *down* block assignments with the knowledge of the movement the defenders will make.

- Previous description is repeated with the offensive personnel not knowing the movement of the defenders.

- Drill continues until all tight ends have had a sufficient number of repetitions in reading the defense and executing the *down* block.

- Drill should be conducted both left and right.

Coaching Points:

- Always check to see that all personnel are aligned correctly and are in their proper stances.

- Instruct all tight ends that their first steps must always be toward the outside hips of the defensive tackles.

- Insist that all tight ends adhere to the following rules:
  - o If the defensive tackle penetrates, the tight end must cut off the penetration using a *gap* technique (head across the front of the defensive tackle) (see diagram A).
  - o If the defensive tackle reacts outside, the tight end gets his head up field and cuts off his pursuit (see diagram B).
  - o If the defensive tackle stays in position, the tight end again uses a *gap* technique (see diagram C).
  - o If the defensive tackle takes an inside charge, the tight end redirects his movement and blocks the linebacker (see diagram D).
  - o The tight end is instructed never to allow the defensive end to penetrate his inside gap (see diagram E).

Safety Considerations:

- It is imperative that proper warm-up precede drill.
- The drill should progress from walk-through to full speed.
- The coach should monitor closely the intensity of the drill.
- Instruct the defenders always to remain alert.

Variations:

- Can be used as a form or live blocking drill.
- Can be used with a post-lead (double team) block.
- Can be used as a defensive end, linebacker, or tackle drill.

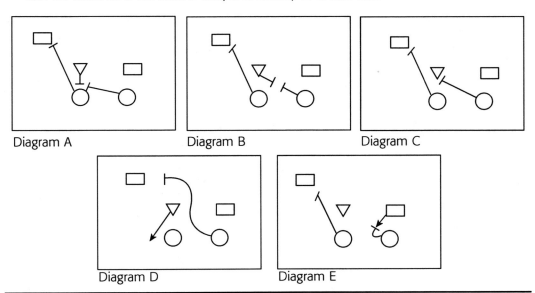

Diagram A Diagram B Diagram C

Diagram D Diagram E

SIX CONES AND A FOOTBALL*

Richard "Dick" Farley
Williams College

Objective: To teach and practice the proper fundamentals and techniques of accelerating in and out of various passing-route break points, catching the football, and eluding a downfield defender.

Equipment Needed: Six cones and a football

Description:

• Place four cones seven-yards apart in the shape of a square. A fifth cone is placed in the middle of the square and a sixth cone is placed seven-yards behind the fifth cone.

• Align a row of tight ends to the right of and behind the cone on the right side of the square. Place a defender in front of the cone positioned behind the square (see diagram).

• The quarterback (coach) is positioned to the left of the line of tight ends and in the normal quarterback-tight end relationship.

• On the quarterback's (coach's) cadence and snap count, the first tight end drives from his stance and sprints past the upfield cone. As he passes the upfield cone, he executes the designated pass route (curl, hitch, or dig) and catches the football thrown by the coach. (See Diagram A for the curl and hitch pattern; see Diagram B for the dig pattern.)

• After catching the football, the tight end turns around and sprints toward the defender positioned in front of the back cone and executes a full-speed double move, beating the defender on the outside.

• The drill continues until all the tight ends have had a sufficient number of repetitions.

• The drill should be conducted with the tight ends running the curl, hitch, and dig patterns from both the left and right side of the squares.

Coaching Points:

• Always check to see that the tight ends are aligned correctly and are in their proper stance.

*Reprinted with permission from 101 Winning Football Drills: From the Legends of the Game by Jerry Tolley

- Instruct all the tight ends to drop their hips, plant their outside foot, and drive the outside knee and elbow toward the midpoint when executing the designated pass route.

- Instruct the tight ends to drive to the middle cone when executing the hitch and curl pattern.

- Insist that the tight ends accelerate in and out of all break points.

- Instruct the tight ends to always watch the football into their hands and to *tuck* it away before sprinting downfield.

Safety Considerations:

- Proper warm-up should precede the drill.

- Helmets should be worn and chinstraps snapped.

- The drill should progress from formwork to full speed.

Variations:

- Can be used as a wide-receiver drill.

- Can be used with any pass-route break point that is a part of the offense's passing scheme.

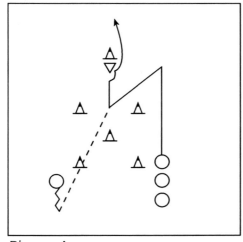

Diagram A

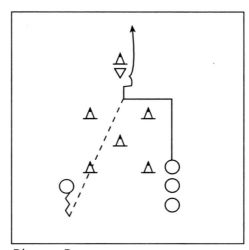

Diagram B

RELEASE DRILL

Paul F. Connor
Southwest Missouri State University, North Central College

Objective: To teach and practice the proper fundamentals and techniques of releasing off the line of scrimmage.

Equipment Needed: Two large blocking dummies, two hand shields, and a football

Description:

- Lay two large blocking dummies three yards apart and at a 45-degree angle from a selected line of scrimmage (see diagram).
- Position a tight end in his stance between the two dummies on the selected line of scrimmage.
- Align a defensive end holding a hand shield head up the tight end. A linebacker holding a hand shield is positioned three yards behind the defensive end.
- Other drill participants stand adjacent to drill area.
- The coach, with football in hand, stands in a normal quarterback pass drop position.
- On coach's cadence and snap count, the tight end drives out of his stance using the designated release technique.
- The two shield holding defenders are instructed to impede the release of the tight end.
- After the tight end executes his release, he then runs a designated pass route and catches the pass thrown by the coach.
- Drill continues until all tight ends have had a sufficient number of line releases both left and right.

Coaching Points:

- Always check to see that tight ends are in their proper stances.
- In executing the line release, instruct tight ends to take a lateral step with the near foot in eluding the defensive end.
- Instruct the tight ends to dip the far shoulder in order to give the defensive ends less body surface to impede their line releases.
- After releasing from the line of scrimmage, insist that tight ends avoid the linebackers and move to their designated pass route as quickly as possible.

Safety Considerations:

- Proper warm-up should precede drill.
- The drill area should be clear of all foreign articles.
- The coach should monitor closely the intensity of the drill.
- Instruct the shield holders not to *jam* the tight end in the head area.
- Instruct the tight end as to the proper fundamentals and techniques in executing the designated line release.

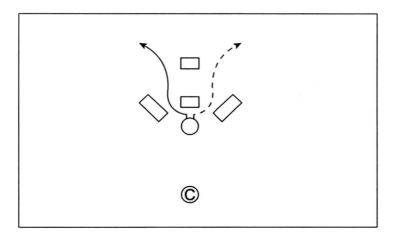

OUTSIDE RELEASE*

Frank L. Girardi
Lycoming College

Objective: To teach and practice the proper fundamentals and techniques in executing the outside release.

Equipment Needed: Hand shield

Description:

- Align a tight end in his stance on a selected line of scrimmage.

- Position a defender, holding a hand shield, in his normal alignment over the tight end.

- Other drill participants stand adjacent to the drill area.

- On the quarterback's (coach's) cadence and snap count, the tight end executes his outside release technique as the defender *jams* him with the hand shield in an effort to prevent his release.

- The drill continues until all the tight ends have had a sufficient number of repetitions using various outside release techniques from both left and right formations.

Coaching Points:

- Always check to see that the tight ends are in their proper stances.

- Instruct the tight ends to first take a lateral step with the outside foot, and then lead through with the inside arm and leg while keeping the shoulders squared.

- The position of the defender should vary from a head-up position to an outside alignment over the tight end.

- After their release from the line of scrimmage, instruct the tight ends to get into their designated pass route as quickly as possible.

*Reprinted with permission from *101 Winning Football Drills: From the Legends of the Game* by Jerry Tolley

Safety Considerations:

- Proper warm-up should precede the drill.

- Helmets should be worn and chinstraps snapped.

- The drill should progress from formwork to live work.

- The coach should monitor closely the intensity of the drill.

- Instruct the defenders not to be overly aggressive in preventing the tight end's release and never to jam the tight end in the head area.

Variations:

- Can be used as a slot-back outside-release drill.

- Can be used as a defensive-end or outside-linebacker drill.

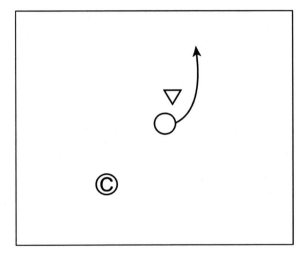

RELEASE TECHNIQUE DRILL

Richard P. "Dick" Scesniak (Deceased)
Iowa State University, University of Utah, University of Washington, New York Giants, University of Wisconsin, Kent State University

Objective: To teach and practice the proper fundamentals and techniques of executing various line releases.

Equipment Needed: Line-spacing strip

Description:

- Place a line-spacing strip on a selected line of scrimmage.

- Position tight ends in their normal alignments on the line-spacing strip. Other tight ends stand behind the first drill performers (see diagram).

- Place a defensive end over each tight end.

- The coach stands behind the defense and signals tight ends as to snap count and the line release technique to be used (head fake counter, overhand swim, and underhand swim).

- On coach's cadence and snap count, the tight ends drive out of their stances and execute the designated release technique. The defensive ends are instructed to prevent the tight ends' releases.

- Drill continues until all tight ends have had a sufficient number of repetitions both from the left and right sides of the formation.

Coaching Points:

- Always check to see that tight ends are aligned correctly and are in their proper stances.

- Insist that the different release techniques be executed correctly.

- The coach should realize that no one particular release technique is best for all tight ends.

Safety Considerations:

- It is imperative that proper warm-up precede drill.
- The drill should progress from formwork to full speed.
- The coach should monitor closely the intensity of the drill.
- Instruct the defensive ends not to be overly aggressive.
- Instruct the tight ends as to the proper fundamentals and techniques in executing the various releases.

Variations:

- Can be used as a wide receiver drill.
- Can be used as a defensive end drill.

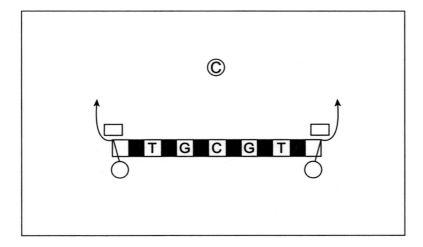

SHOULDER TURN/EYE CONCENTRATION

Jim Dickey
University of Houston, Oklahoma State University, University of Oklahoma,
University of Kansas, University of North Carolina, Kansas State University,
University of Florida, University of Southern Mississippi

Objective: To teach and practice the proper fundamentals and techniques of catching the football with special emphasis on concentration. Incorporated are skills related to getting the head and shoulders around quickly and locating the football.

Equipment Needed: Footballs (with tips painted different colors)

Description:

- Position a passer holding a football on a selected line of scrimmage.
- Align a tight end with his back to the passer 15 yards upfield and at a 45-degree angle from the passer (see diagram).
- Other tight ends stand adjacent to the drill area.
- On quarterback's command, left or right, the tight end turns only his head and shoulders in the direction indicated (feet remain planted).
- The quarterback is instructed to pass the football at any time prior to the verbal command.
- The tight end now locates the flight of the pass, calls out the color on the tip of the football, makes the catch, and tucks the football away.
- Drill continues until all tight ends have had a sufficient number of repetitions.
- Drill should be conducted with passes thrown both to the left and right of the tight end.

Coaching Points:

- Instruct the tight ends to thrust their elbows back in the direction of the turn.
- Make sure that all tight ends keep their feet planted throughout the drill.
- Insist that tight ends tuck the footballs away properly.

Safety Considerations:

- Proper warm-up should precede drill.

- Helmets and shoulder pads should be worn. Chinstraps should be snapped.

- Instruct alternating drill participants always to remain alert.

Variations:

- Can be used with the tight end taking two steps forward prior to the head and shoulder turn.

- Can be used with varying distances between the quarterback and tight ends.

- Can be used as a wide receiver drill.

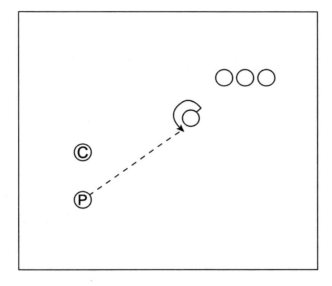

TWO-LEVEL RELEASE*

Jim Tressel
University of Akron, University of Miami (OH), Youngstown State University,
The Ohio State University
National Champions: Youngstown State 1991, 1993, 1994, and 1997,
Ohio State 2002
National Coach of the Year: Youngstown State 1991, 1993, 1994, and 1997,
Ohio State 2002

Objective: To teach and practice the proper fundamentals and techniques in executing line releases and linebacker-level releases. Incorporated are skills related to pass catching and concentration.

Equipment Needed: Four arm shields, a cone, and footballs

Description:

- Position a tight end in his stance on a selected line of scrimmage. A cone is placed at the center position.

- Defenders holding arm shields are positioned one over the outside shoulder of the tight end, another at the onside linebacker position, and two others at the end of the designated pass route (hook pattern - see diagram).

- Other tight ends stand adjacent to the drill area.

- A coach holding a football is aligned behind the center (cone) at the appropriate quarterback pass drop alignment.

- On the coach's cadence and snap count, the tight end releases off the line of scrimmage executing either the *rip*, *swim*, or *counter-rip/swim* technique as the defensive end jams the tight end in an effort to prevent the release.

- After gaining a release from the line of scrimmage, the tight end continues upfield and executes the *rip-and-drive*, the *stick-and-club*, or *speed* technique on the linebacker. The linebacker who is reading the tight end's release move to his outside *jams* the tight end in an effort to prevent his release at the second level.

- After clearing the linebacker the tight end continues upfield running the designated *hook* pattern. As the tight end comes out of his pass route break point, he drives between the two downfield defenders, and the coach passes him the pass as the two defenders attempt to disrupt the tight end by *jamming* him as he makes the catch.

*Reprinted with permission from *101 Winning Football Drills: From the Legends of the Game* by Jerry Tolley

- After the catch is made, the tight end *tucks* the football away and sprints upfield.

- The drill continues until all the tight ends have had a sufficient number of repetitions from both the left and right alignments.

Coaching Points:

- Always check to see that the tight ends are aligned correctly and are in their proper stances.

- In executing the *rip* technique, instruct the tight ends to take a lateral step to the side of the release and then drive their release-side shoulder under the defensive end and *power up* through the level.

- In executing the *swim* technique, instruct the tight ends to pin the defensive end's release-side elbow toward his hip and swim with the opposite arm over the top.

- In executing the *counter/rip-swim technique,* instruct the tight ends to head-and-shoulder fake the defensive end in the opposite direction before executing the release.

- In executing the *rip-and-drive technique,* instruct the tight ends to execute a rip while driving through the linebacker.

- In executing the *stick-and-club technique,* instruct the tight ends to head fake opposite and *club* the linebacker's arm to the hip before *ripping* upfield.

- In executing the *speed* technique, instruct the tight ends to beat the linebacker to the release point.

- Instruct the tight ends to always maintain a vertical push upfield and not to get re-routed by the defensive end or linebacker.

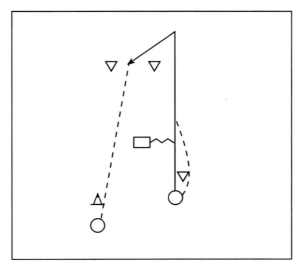

Safety Considerations:

- Proper warm-up should precede drill.
- The drill area should be clear of all foreign articles.
- The coach should monitor closely the intensity of the drill.
- Instruct all the defenders not to be overly aggressive and not to *jam* the tight ends in the head area.
- Instruct the tight ends as to the proper fundamentals and techniques in executing the different releases.
- The drill should progress from walk through to full speed.

Variation:

- Can be used as a defensive-end and strong-side linebacker drill.

7

Wide Receiver Drills

SQUARE DRILL

Richard "Rich" Rodriguez
Clemson University, Tulane University, Salem University, Glenville State University, West Virginia University
National Coach of the Year: Glenville State 1993

Objective: To teach and practice the proper fundamentals and techniques of coming out of a vertical release and into a designated pass cut at full speed.

Equipment Needed: Five cones and footballs

Description:

- Place four cones five yards apart to form a square. A fifth cone is placed in the center of the square.

- Position a row of wide receivers in a straight line behind and to the right of the designated cone (see diagram).

- The coach is positioned downfield from the row of receivers to watch the receivers' release while focusing on the receivers' eyes.

- A manager is positioned over the football at the center position.

- On coach's cadence and snap count, the manager simulates the center snap, and the first receiver drives out of his stance and sprints to the downfield cone while looking at the coach.

- When the receiver passes the downfield cone he executes a 90-degree cut around the cone. (As the receiver makes the cut, he *snaps* his head toward the manager and drives at full speed underneath the third cone.) The manager does *not* pass the football.

- The drill continues until all the receivers have had a sufficient number of repetitions from both the left and right side of the front cones.

Coaching Points:

- Always check to see that receivers are in a *perfect* stance.

- Instruct the receivers to explode from their stance with the head up and with the eyes focused on the downfield coach.

- Insist that the receivers sprint full speed into and out of the 90-degree pass cut.

- When executing the 90-degree cut, instruct the receivers to turn their heads and simultaneously pull their inside elbows before turning their bodies.

- Insist that all receivers finish the drill in a full sprint.

Safety Considerations:

- It is imperative that proper warm-up precedes drill.

- The drill area should be clear of all foreign articles.

- Helmets should be worn with chinstraps snapped.

- The coach should monitor closely the intensity of the drill.

Variations:

- Can be run with the manager (center) aligned in any of three positions (see diagram).

- Can be used with the manager passing the football to the receivers after the pass cut is executed.

- Can be used with the manager throwing a tennis ball to the receivers (the tennis ball is used in the off-season).

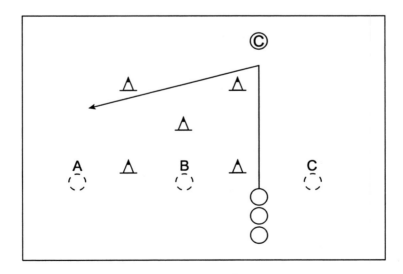

CONE DRILL*

PAUL "BEAR" BRYANT (DECEASED)
[Drill submitted by Ray Perkins]
Vanderbilt University, University of Maryland, University of Kentucky,
Texas A&M University, University of Alabama
National Champions: Alabama 1961, 1964, 1965, 1973, 1978, and 1979
National Coach of the Year: Alabama 1961, 1971, and 1973
College Football Hall of Fame: 1986
Amos Alonzo Stagg Award: 1983
AFCA President: 1972

Objective: To teach and practice the proper fundamentals and techniques of coming off a pass cut at full speed and catching the football.

Equipment Needed: Four cones and footballs

Description:

- Align four cones 10-yards apart in a square as shown in the diagram.

- Position all receivers in a straight line behind one of the cones.

- The coach stands in the middle of the drill area holding a football.

- On the coach's command (raising the football), the first receiver drives from his stance and sprints to and executes a 90-degree turn around the first cone. As he makes the turn, he looks for a pass thrown by the coach.

- This procedure continues around the remaining two cones with the coach throwing the receiver the pass after any one of his 90-degree cuts.

- The drill continues until all the receivers have had a sufficient number of repetitions.

- The drill should be conducted with the receivers running both clockwise and counterclockwise around the square.

*Reprinted with permission from 101 Winning Football Drills: From the Legends of the Game by Jerry Tolley

Coaching Points:

- Make sure that the receivers plant and cut off their outside foot in executing each 90-degree turn.

- Insist that all the receivers run at full speed and only come under control approximately two and one-half yards from each cone.

- Emphasize the importance of exploding off the cut and getting the head around as quickly as possible.

- Insist that the receivers catch all the passes with their hands.

Safety Considerations:

- Proper warm-up should precede the drill.

- Helmets should be worn with chinstraps snapped.

Variations:

- Can be used to practice the 45-degree comeback pattern.

- Can be used as a tight end and running back drill.

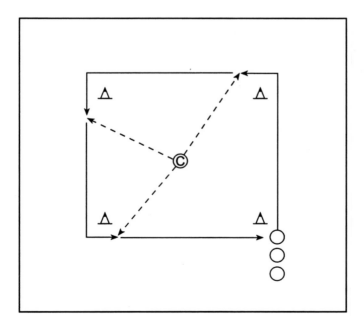

COMEBACK AND CONCENTRATION DRILL

Ted Tollner

University of Southern California, Los Angeles Rams, San Diego Chargers, Buffalo Bills, San Diego State University, San Francisco 49ers

Objective: To teach and practice the proper fundamentals and techniques of catching the football. Incorporated are skills related to proper footwork, body control, hand position, eye contact, and concentration.

Equipment Needed: Footballs

Description:

- Align a row of wide receivers at a position that will allow them to take the last two steps before initiating the final cut of a designated pass route.
- A quarterback, holding a football, is positioned in the proper pass drop relationship to the receivers.
- The coach stands adjacent to the catch area and watches the eyes of the receiver.
- On quarterback's command, the first wide receiver takes the last two steps preceding his final cut and then breaks for the pass thrown by the quarterback.
- The receiver catches the pass, tucks it away, and sprints for the goal line.
- Drill continues until alternating receivers have had a sufficient number of catches at various ending patterns.
- Drill should be conducted both left and right and from various field positions.

Coaching Points:

- Instruct the receivers to always come out of their breaks with their hips low and their weight on the balls of their feet.
- The receivers should follow the flight of the football until it is secured in their hands.
- Make sure receivers do not round-off their pass patterns.
- The pace of the drill should be controlled so that proper techniques can be emphasized.

Safety Considerations:

- Proper warm-up should precede drill.
- Drill area should be clear of all foreign articles.
- Helmets should be worn with chinstraps snapped.

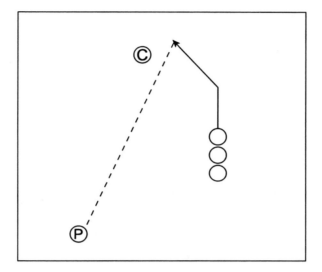

NET-FLASH DRILL*

Ken W. Hatfield
United States Military Academy, University of Tennessee, University of Florida,
United States Air Force Academy, University of Arkansas,
Clemson University, Rice University
National Coach of the Year: Air Force 1983
Fellowship of Christian Athletes Grant Teaff Coach of the Year: Air Force 2001
AFCA President: 2004

Objective: To teach and practice the proper fundamentals and techniques of catching the football with special emphasis on hand-eye coordination, concentration, and protecting the football.

Equipment Needed: Goal post net, two hand shields, and footballs

Description:

- Position a receiver in the middle of the end zone facing a netted goalpost.

- Shield holders are positioned on both sides of the receiver.

- The quarterback (coach) stands ten yards from the receiver.

- Alternating drill participants stand adjacent to the drill area.

- On the quarterback's (coach's) command, the receiver executes a 180-degree turn and catches the pass thrown by the quarterback.

- The receiver now tucks the football under the arm opposite the way he turned (if receiver turns to his right, the football is tucked under the left arm) as the shield holder on the side of the football *jams* him with his shield.

- The drill continues until all the receivers have had a sufficient number of catches turning to both their left and right.

Coaching Points:

- Instruct all the receivers to turn their heads first and then their bodies.

- Make sure that the receivers watch the football into their hands.

- Insist that the receivers tuck and cover the football completely after each reception is made.

*Reprinted with permission from *101 Winning Football Drills: From the Legends of the Game* by Jerry Tolley

Safety Considerations:

- Proper warm-up should precede the drill.

- Helmets should be worn with chinstraps snapped.

- Full equipment should be worn.

- Instruct the shield holder not to *jam* the receiver in the head area.

Variations:

- Can be used as a tight end and running back drill.

- Can be used as a defensive back, linebacker, and defensive end drill.

- Passes can be thrown at different heights and with varying velocities.

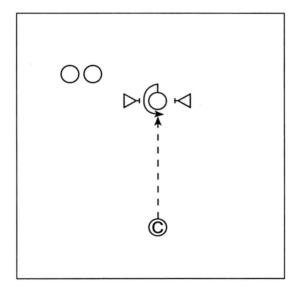

CONCENTRATION DRILL

Don Ault
Marshall University, Bethany College, Slippery Rock University

Objective: To teach and practice the proper fundamentals and techniques of concentrating when catching the football.

Equipment Needed: Three hand shields and footballs (with one-inch numbers painted on each of the football panels)

Description:

- Align three shield holders three yards apart forming an equilateral triangle (see diagram).
- Position a row of wide receivers five yards to the right of the triangle.
- The coach (passer), holding a football, stands five yards to the left of the triangle.
- On coach's command, the first receiver jogs to the center of the triangle and catches the soft high pass thrown by the coach.
- As the receiver catches the pass, he calls out the number painted on the football as the three shield holders *jam* him with their shields.
- Drill continues until all receivers have had a sufficient number of repetitions jogging from both the left and right of the triangle.

Coaching Points:

- Instruct the receivers to catch the football with authority.
- Make sure the receivers follow the flight of the pass until it is secured in their hands.
- Make sure the receivers call out the correct number with each pass caught.
- Emphasis should be placed on concentrating when catching each pass.

Safety Considerations:

- Proper warm-up should precede drill.
- Full equipment should always be worn and chinstraps should be snapped.
- The coach should monitor closely the intensity of the drill.
- Instruct the shield holders never to *jam* the receiver in the head area.

Variations:

- Can be used as a tight end and running back drill.
- Can be used as an interception drill by defensive personnel.

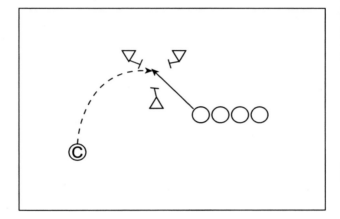

TWO-STEP-CURL ANGLE AND CATCH DRILL

Steve Smyte
American River College, Sacramento River City Gamblers,
Sacramento Gold Miners (CFL), University of California-Davis, Boise State University

Objective: To teach and practice the proper fundamentals and techniques in executing the last four steps in the execution of the curl pattern.

Equipment Needed: Footballs

Description:

- Position a coach (passer), holding a football, on the hash mark of a selected line of scrimmage.

- Align a wide receiver on the near sideline and two steps from the yard line 10 yards upfield from the passer. The receiver's outside foot should be forward.

- Other drill participants stand adjacent to the drill area.

- On passer's command, the receiver executes the next four steps as follows:
  - On step one, the receiver steps forward with the inside foot.
  - On step two, the receiver steps forward and *plants* his outside foot at the midpoint of the sideline and yard line 10 yards upfield from the passer.
  - On step three, the receiver drives back toward the passer with the inside foot and gets *ready* to catch the pass.
  - On step four, the receiver steps toward the passer with his outside foot and catches the pass thrown by the passer, *secures* it away, and sprints upfield for 15 yards.

- Drill continues until all receivers have had a sufficient number of repetitions.

- Drill should be conducted from both the left and right sidelines.

Coaching Points:

- Always check to see that receivers are aligned correctly—two steps from the midpoint of the sideline and the upfield 10-yard line. Also check to see that the outside foot is forward.

- When taking step one, with the inside foot, instruct the receivers to *pump* their arms, not to overstride and to *gather* themselves by lowering the hips.

- When taking step two, with the outside foot, emphasize the importance of *planting* the foot hard in preparation for step three.

- When taking step three, instruct the receivers to drive back toward the passer with the inside foot and with the knees flexed and the shoulders *squared* and facing the passer.

- When taking step four, instruct the receivers again to drive back toward the passer with the outside foot and to stay low and concentrate on making the catch.

- Emphasize the importance of catching and *securing* the football and sprinting upfield for 15 yards.

Safety Considerations:

- Proper warm-up should precede drill.

- The drill area (including sideline areas) should be clear of all foreign articles.

- Helmets should be worn with the chinstraps snapped.

- Instruct returning pass receivers to stay clear of the drill area.

Variations:

- Can be used in the execution of the next four steps of other pass patterns.

- Can be used as a tight end drill.

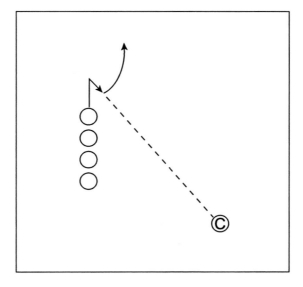

RELEASE DRILL*

J. Hayden Fry
Baylor University, University of Arkansas, Southern Methodist University,
North Texas State University, University of Iowa
National Coach of the Year: Iowa 1981
College Football Hall of Fame: 2003
AFCA President: 1993
Amos Alonzo Stagg Award: 2005

Objective: To teach and practice the proper fundamentals and techniques in releasing from the line of scrimmage.

Equipment Needed: Hand shield and footballs

Description:

- Align receivers five-yards apart on a selected line of scrimmage.

- A defender with a hand shield is positioned at various depths either inside, outside, or head-up each receiver. He is instructed to prevent the release of the receiver.

- On the coach's cadence and snap count, the receiver executes one of four release techniques (A - inside, B - outside, C- roll-out, and D - roll-in) as designated by the coach (see diagram).

- After the designated release technique is executed, the receiver carries out his regular blocking or pass play assignment.

- The drill continues until all the receivers have executed a sufficient number of line releases.

- The drill should be conducted from both left and right formations.

Coaching Points:

- Always check to see that the receivers are aligned correctly and are in their proper stances.

- Instruct the receivers to turn inside and to watch for an imaginary ball snap.

- Insist that the receivers drive off the line of scrimmage as dictated by the depth and alignment of the defenders.

- Instruct all the receivers as to the desired techniques and fundamentals of executing the four designated releases.

*Reprinted with permission from *101 Winning Football Drills: From the Legends of the Game* by Jerry Tolley

Safety Considerations:

- Proper warm-up should precede the drill.
- Maintain a minimum distance of five-yards between each pair of paired drill participants.
- Helmets should be worn and chinstraps snapped.
- The coach should monitor closely the intensity of the drill.
- Instruct the defender not to *jam* the receiver in the head area.

Variations:

- Can be used as a form or live drill.
- Can be used simulating different down-and-distance situations.
- Can be used as a tight end release drill.

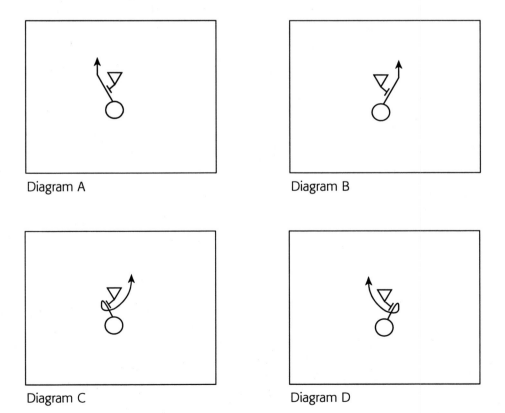

Diagram A

Diagram B

Diagram C

Diagram D

DISTRACTION DRILL

Ben S. Martin (Deceased)
United States Naval Academy, University of Virginia, United States Air Force Academy
AFCA President 1977

Objective: To teach and practice the proper techniques and fundamentals of catching a football during contact. Incorporated are skills related to concentration.

Equipment Needed: Hand shields and footballs

Description:

- The coach should designate all receivers as either distractors, shield holders, or receivers.

- Align designated receivers on a selected yard line at the left hash mark. Distractors are positioned in a corresponding alignment on the right hash marks two yards in front of the selected line of scrimmage. Shield holders are also placed at the right hash mark but two yards behind the selected line of scrimmage (see diagram).

- The coach stands 15 yards in front and at the midpoint between the two hash marks.

- On coach's command, a receiver and distractor run toward each other at a controlled pace. As their paths begin to cross, the coach throws the pass. The distractor waves his arms in front of the flight of the ball and the receiver catches the football.

- The shield holder is instructed to delay his start and to time his movement so he can *jam* the receiver just after the reception is made.

- Drill continues until all receivers have had a sufficient number of repetitions from both left and right alignments.

- Receivers, distractors, and shield holders can be interchanged at the discretion of the coach.

Coaching Points:

- Make sure receivers catch the football in their hands if possible.

- Instruct receivers to *tuck* footballs away as soon as catches are made.

- Distractors should be instructed not to touch the football.

- The coach should throw the football at various heights and speeds.
- Make sure the shield holders delay their starts so they can *jam* the receivers after the reception is made.

Safety Considerations:

- Proper warm-up should precede drill.
- Drill area should be clear of all foreign articles.
- Helmets should be worn with chinstraps snapped.
- Instruct the shield holders not to jam the receiver in the head area.

Variations:

- Can be used without shield holders.
- Can be used as a tight end and running back drill.
- Can be used as a defensive interception drill.

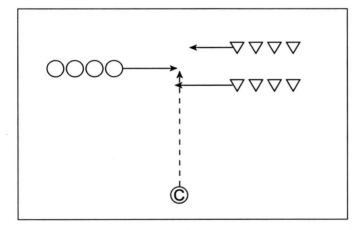

STALK-BLOCKING DRILL*

Dr. Gene A. Carpenter
Adams State College, Millersville University

Objective: To teach and practice the proper fundamentals and techniques in the execution of the stalk block. Incorporated are skills of reaction and quickness.

Equipment Needed: Hand shield

Description:

- Align receivers in a straight line perpendicular to a selected line of scrimmage. The alignment should be relative to the offensive formation and such that the receivers are in the best position to block for the particular play called.

- A defender with a hand shield is positioned five yards in front of the first receiver.

- The coach stands behind the first receiver (see diagram).

- On the coach's cadence and snap count, the receiver drives out of his stance forcing the defender into his backpedal. The receiver works for a position one-yard outside the defender.

- The defender continues his retreat until the coach signals him to initiate his run support either straight ahead or to the outside.

- As the defender approaches the line of scrimmage, the receiver executes his stalk block.

- If the defender attacks straight-ahead (diagram A), the receiver must stop his penetration; and if he attacks to the outside (diagram B), the receiver drives him to the sideline.

- The drill continues until all the receivers have executed a sufficient number of stalk blocks.

- The drill should be conducted from both the left and right sides of the field and from left and right formations.

*Reprinted with permission from *101 Winning Football Drills: From the Legends of the Game* by Jerry Tolley

Coaching Points:

- Always check to see that the receivers are aligned correctly and are in their proper stances.

- Instruct the receivers to run-off the defender as far as possible.

- Make sure the receivers are under complete control as they execute their stalk blocks.

Safety Considerations:

- Proper warm-up is imperative with this drill.

- The drill area should be clear of all foreign articles.

- The drill should progress from form blocking to live blocking.

- The coach should monitor closely the intensity of the drill.

- Instruct the shield holder not to *jam* the receiver in the head area.

Variations:

- Can be used as a form or live-blocking drill.

- Can be used as a defensive back drill.

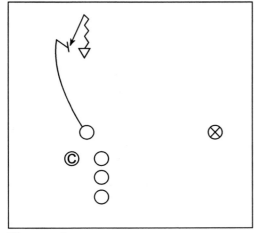

Diagram A

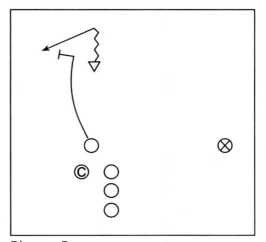

Diagram B

DOWNFIELD STALK BLOCK

Henry T. Trevathan
East Carolina University, Elon University, North Carolina State University,
Bridgewater College

Objective: To teach and practice the proper fundamentals and techniques in the execution of the stalk block.

Equipment Needed: None

Description:

- Align receivers in a straight line behind a selected line of scrimmage. Their alignment should be relative to the offensive formation with a split indicating a deep pass pattern to that side (13 to 15 yards wide).

- A cornerback is placed at varying run-support alignments (see diagram).

- The coach stands in a position that best allows him to observe the block.

- On coach's command, the first receiver sprints from his stance driving the defender as far downfield as possible.

- The cornerback, at his discretion, breaks toward the line of scrimmage at different run-support angles.

- When the defender shows run support, the receiver stops his sprint and positions himself at an outside 30-degree angle and three yards in front of the defender.

- The defender is instructed to get past the receiver either by running around or over him.

- The receiver now executes his *stalk* block technique by cutting left and right while maintaining a position that opposes the corner back's run support. The position is one in which the cornerback would have to go through the receiver to get to the ballcarrier. If early contact becomes imminent, the receiver should meet the contact while maintaining balance as he continues to retreat. When the corner back makes his final effort to reach the ballcarrier the receiver should *take the charge* (as in *taking the charge* in basketball).

- Drill continues until all receivers have had a sufficient number of repetitions.

- Drill should be conducted from both left and right formation alignments and from various field positions.

Coaching Points:

- Always check to see that receivers are aligned correctly and are in their proper stances.

- Insist that all receivers sprint out of their stances and drive off the defender.

- Instruct the receivers to be under complete control as the stalk block is being executed.

- When the alignment of the receiver takes him to within three yards of the sideline, he should try for an inside 30-degree angle relationship to the defender.

Safety Considerations:

- Proper warm-up should precede drill.

- Drill area (including sideline areas) should be clear of all foreign articles.

- Drill should progress from form blocking to live blocking.

- The coach should monitor closely the intensity of the drill.

- Under no circumstances is the defender allowed to abuse the receiver when the receiver is *taking the charge*.

Variations:

- Can be used as a form or live blocking drill.

- Can be used with a ballcarrier.

- Can be used with a quarterback and have receiver fake a *stalk* block and run a pass pattern.

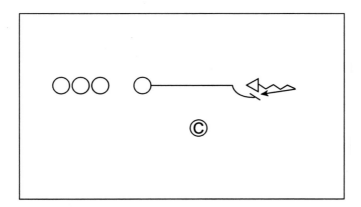

SWIM-RELEASE DRILL*

Don Nehlen
University of Cincinnati, University of Michigan, Bowling Green State University,
West Virginia University
National Coach of the Year: West Virginia 1988 and 1993
AFCA President: 1997

Objective: To teach and practice the proper fundamentals and techniques in the execution of a quick release off the line of scrimmage against a squat corner. Also incorporated are skills of driving out of a stance.

Equipment Needed: Cone, hand shield, and footballs

Description:

- Align wide receivers in a straight line behind a selected line of scrimmage. Their alignment should be in the proper relationship to the formation and the particular play to be run.

- A defensive squat corner with a hand shield lines up in his regular position six yards in front of the first receiver.

- A cone is placed six yards behind the defender.

- On the coach's cadence and snap count, the first wide receiver drives out of his stance and moves directly toward the squat corner.

- When reaching the corner, the receiver plants his release-side foot and punches the corner with the release-side hand. He then carries his opposite hand over the shoulder of the defender in a swimming motion as the inside leg crosses over and past the defender's hip.

- The receiver now completes the swim move and sprints to the cone.

- The drill continues until all the receivers have had a sufficient number of repetitions.

- The drill should be conducted from both the left and right sides of the field and from left and right formations.

---

*Reprinted with permission from 101 Winning Football Drills: From the Legends of the Game by Jerry Tolley

Coaching Points:

- Always check to see that the receivers are aligned correctly and are in their proper stances.

- Insist that all the receivers drive out of their stances low and fast and without false stepping.

- Instruct the receivers to turn their shoulders as they execute the swim technique in an effort to reduce their hitting surface.

- Emphasize the importance of sprinting to the cone after the swim technique is executed.

Safety Considerations:

- It is imperative that proper warm-up precede this drill.

- The drill should progress from form to live work.

- The coach should monitor closely the intensity of the drill.

- Instruct the shield holder not to *jam* the receiver in the head area.

Variations:

- Can be used as a form or live drill.

- Can be used in teaching all pass routes.

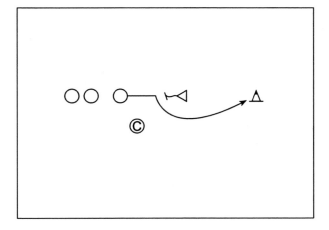

GREAT CATCH DRILL

Davis H. Buescher
Austin Peay State University, University of Richmond, Baylor University

Objective: To teach and practice the proper fundamentals and techniques in adjusting to and catching a poorly-thrown pass.

Equipment Needed: Footballs

Description:

- Align all receivers in a straight line five yards from the sideline and behind a selected line of scrimmage.
- The quarterback (coach) is positioned in his normal alignment in a quarterback-receiver relationship (see diagram).
- On quarterback's (coach's) cadence and snap count, the first receiver drives out of his stance and runs downfield at three-quarter speed looking over his inside shoulder.
- The quarterback (coach) now throws the football over the receiver's outside shoulder forcing him to adjust to the poorly thrown football and thus making a *great* catch.
- Drill continues until all receivers have had a sufficient number of repetitions.
- Drill should be conducted from both the left and right sidelines.

Coaching Points:

- Always check to see that receivers are in their proper stances.
- Instruct the receivers to *whip* the head and shoulders to the outside when adjusting to passes thrown over their outside shoulder.

Safety Considerations:

- Proper warm-up should precede drill.

- Drill area (including sideline areas) should be clear of all foreign articles.

- Helmets should be worn with chinstraps snapped.

- Instruct returning drill participants to stay clear of the drill area.

Variations:

- Can be used with the quarterback underthrowing the football to a receiver running on a fly pattern.

- Can be used with a variety of pass patterns (sideline, curl, etc.).

- Can be used as a tight end drill.

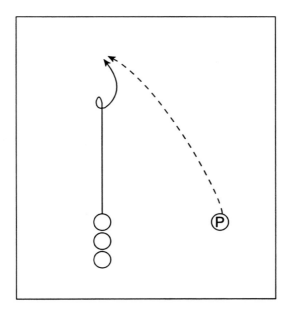

ACCURACY AND CONCENTRATION*

Billy Joe

University of Maryland, Philadelphia Eagles, Cheyney State University,
Central State University (OH), Florida A&M University
National Champions: Central State 1990 and 1992
National Black College Champions: Central State 1983, 1984, 1985, 1986,
1987, 1988, 1989, 1990, 1991, and 1992; Florida A&M 1998
National Coach of the Year: Central State 1992
National Black College Coach of the Year: Central State 1986, 1987,
1988, 1989, and 1990; Florida A&M 1996
AFCA President: 1995

Objective: To teach and practice the proper mechanics of throwing the sideline pass with accuracy for the quarterback, and to teach and practice the proper sideline footwork, body control, and concentration while catching the football for wide receivers.

Equipment Needed: Footballs

Description:

- Align a wide receiver at the halfway point of his sideline pass route on a selected line of scrimmage (see diagram).

- Align a quarterback with a football in hand in the proper pass-drop relationship with the wide receiver. (Remember that the receiver's drill starting point is already halfway through his sideline-pass route.)

- Other drill participants stand adjacent to the drill area.

- On the quarterback's command, the wide receiver takes the last three steps of his downfield run, breaks for the sideline, and looks for the pass thrown by the quarterback.

- As the pass approaches, the receiver concentrates on catching the football and keeping his feet in bounds.

- The wide receiver coach is positioned in the catch area of the sidelines and monitors the catch.

- The drill continues until all the receivers have had a sufficient number of repetitions from both the left and the right sidelines.

*Reprinted with permission from 101 Winning Football Drills: From the Legends of the Game by Jerry Tolley

Coaching Points:

- Make sure quarterbacks' pass drops are executed correctly.
- Make sure all quarterbacks practice the proper mechanics in throwing all passes.
- Instruct the quarterbacks to look off the receiver until his final drop step is made.
- Instruct the receivers to concentrate fully, maintain complete body control, catch the football with the hands, and to stay in bounds.

Safety Considerations:

- Full equipment should be worn.
- The drill area (including sideline areas) should be clear of all foreign articles.

Variation:

- Can be executed from the shotgun formation.

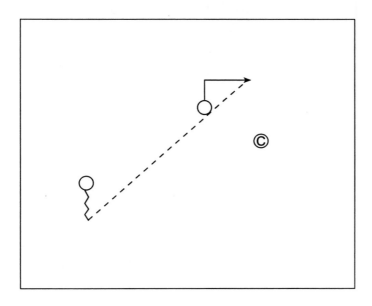

LONG BALL DRILL

Steve Charles Sloan

Vanderbilt University, Texas Tech University, University of Mississippi, Duke University

Objective: To teach and practice the proper fundamentals and techniques of catching the long pass.

Equipment Needed: Footballs

Description:

- Align all wide receivers in a straight line eight yards from the sideline and behind a selected line of scrimmage. The first drill participant places his back foot on the selected line of scrimmage.

- A defensive back is positioned one foot to the inside of the first receiver. The defender's front foot placed on the selected line of scrimmage.

- A quarterback, holding a football lines up in his regular position and in the normal quarterback-receiver relationship.

- On quarterback's cadence and snap count, both receiver and defender sprint downfield. The receiver's pass route should take him to within three yards of the sideline.

- After taking a five-step to seven-step pass drop, the quarterback throws a pass 30 to 40 yards downfield over the receiver's outside shoulder.

- The receiver catches the football, tucks it away, and sprints for the goal line.

- The defender is instructed to intercept or break up the pass.

- Drill continues until all receivers have had a sufficient number of repetitions.

- The drill should be conducted from both the left and right sidelines.

Coaching Points:

- Always check to see that all receivers are aligned correctly and are in their proper stances.

- Make sure all receivers stay at least three yards from sidelines.

- Emphasize the importance of making the *big* catch.

- Instruct the receivers to catch under thrown passes with thumbs in.
- Instruct the receivers that the defender must not intercept the pass.
- Insist that the drill be conducted at full speed.

Safety Considerations:

- Proper warm-up should precede drill.
- Drill area (including sideline areas) should be clear of all foreign articles.
- Drill should progress from form work to live work.
- Instruct returning drill participants to stay clear of drill area.

Variations:

- Can be used as a tight end drill.
- Can be used as a defensive back drill.

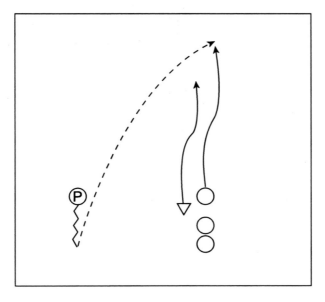

OUT ADJUSTMENT DRILL

Mike C. Gottfried

Morehead State University, Youngstown State University, University of Cincinnati, University of Arizona, Murray State University, University of Kansas, University of Pittsburgh

Objective: To teach and practice the proper fundamentals and techniques of reading defensive coverage and adjusting the out route accordingly.

Equipment Needed: Footballs

Description:

- Align a center, a quarterback and a receiver in an out route alignment over the football on a selected line of scrimmage (see diagram).

- Alternating receivers stand adjacent to their drill area.

- A cornerback (coach) and strong safety are positioned in their normal alignment over the offense.

- Prior to cadence and ball snap, the secondary will show a particular coverage. This coverage may or may not be the one that is implemented.

- On cadence and ball snap, the quarterback takes a seven-step pass drop and the receiver drives out of his stance and runs his out route. The pattern is adjusted according to the four coverages (as shown in the diagrams): two-deep zone (A), three-deep zone (B), two-deep man (C), and man (D).

- Drill continues until all receivers have had a sufficient number of repetitions.

- Drill should be conducted from both left and right formations and to both the flanker and split end.

Coaching Points:

- Always check to see that receivers are aligned correctly and are in their proper stances.

- Insist that all receivers drive out of their stances low and hard.

- Make sure that the receivers adjust their pattern according to the secondary coverage.

- Instruct the defenders to vary their secondary coverages.

- Insist that the drill be conducted at full speed.

Safety Considerations:

- Proper warm-up should precede drill.
- Drill area (including sideline areas) should be clear of all foreign articles.
- Helmets should be worn and chinstraps snapped.

Variations:

- Can be used as a live drill by substituting a cornerback for the coach.
- Can be used with other adjusting pass routes.
- Can incorporate other offensive and defensive personnel.
- Can be used as a quarterback *read* drill.
- Can be used as a defensive back drill.

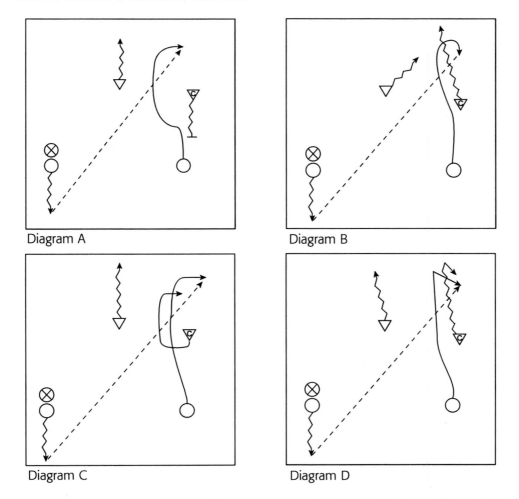

Diagram A

Diagram B

Diagram C

Diagram D

FOCUS*

Joe Glenn
Northern Arizona University, University of South Dakota, Doane College,
University of Northern Colorado, University of Montana, University of Wyoming
National Champions: Northern Colorado 1996 and 1997; Montana 2001
National Coach of the Year: Northern Colorado 1996 and 1997; Montana 2000

Objective: To teach and practice the proper fundamentals and techniques of catching the football. Incorporated are skills related to concentration and looking the ball into the hands.

Equipment Needed: Tennis balls or footballs

Description:

Phase I

- Align a row of wide receivers five yards from a designated sideline and behind a selected line of scrimmage (see diagram A).

- Position a quarterback (coach) on the rear hash mark with a tennis ball in hand and on the same line of scrimmage as the receiver.

- On the coach's cadence and snap count, the first wide receiver drives out of his stance and runs a one-half to three-quarter-speed fly pattern looking for the thrown tennis ball over his inside shoulder.

- The coach throws the tennis ball 10- to 15-yards downfield and the receiver catches the ball with two hands.

- The drill continues until all the wide receivers have had a sufficient number of repetitions catching the football from both the left and right sidelines.

Phase II

- Align a row of receivers in a straight line on a selected line of scrimmage and on the near numbers (see diagram B).

- Position a quarterback (coach) with a tennis ball in hand 15-yards downfield and 15-yards horizontal to the row of wide receivers.

- On the coach's cadence and snap count, the first receiver drives out of his stance and runs a one-half to three-quarter-speed crossing pattern and catches the tennis ball thrown by the coach.

*Reprinted with permission from 101 Winning Football Drills: From the Legends of the Game by Jerry Tolley

- The drill continues until all the receivers have had a sufficient number of repetitions catching the tennis ball from both the left and the right.

Coaching Points:

- Always check to see that the wide receivers are in their proper stance.
- The coach should throw the tennis ball at game speed.
- Instruct the receivers to see their fingers catch the tennis ball.
- Insist that the receivers catch the tennis ball with the fingers of both hands.

Safety Considerations:

- Proper warm-up should precede the drill.
- The drill area (including sideline areas) should be clear of all foreign articles.
- Helmets should be worn and chinstraps snapped.
- Instruct the returning drill participants to stay clear of drill area (including sideline areas).

Variations:

- Can be performed using a football in place of the tennis ball.
- Can be used as a tight end drill.
- Can be used as a defensive back drill.

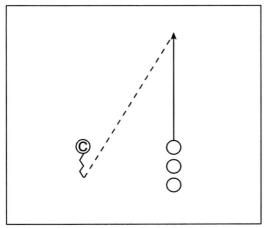

Diagram A

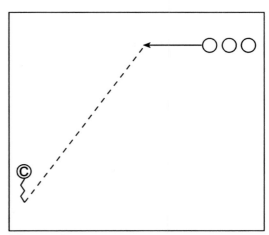

Diagram B

ONE-HAND CATCH

Brian G. Burke
The College of William and Mary, North Carolina State University,
University of Virginia, Ohio University

Objective: To teach and practice the proper fundamentals and techniques in making a one-hand reception. Incorporated are skills related to confidence building, concentration, and sideline awareness. Stance and start are also important.

Equipment Needed: Footballs

Description:

- Align all wide receivers in a straight line five yards from the sideline and behind a selected line of scrimmage.

- The quarterback (coach), holding a football, is also aligned on the selected line of scrimmage and on the near side hash mark.

- On quarterback's cadence and snap count, the first receiver drives out of his stance and runs a one-half to three-quarter speed *fly* pattern while looking over his inside shoulder.

- The quarterback (coach) passes the football downfield and the receiver makes the one-handed catch (passes are caught with the left hand when running down the left sideline and with the right hand when running down the right sideline).

- Drill continues until all receivers have executed a sufficient number of one-handed catches.

- Drill should be conducted both from the left and right sidelines.

Coaching Points:

- Always check to see that receivers are aligned correctly and are in their proper stances.

- Insist that receivers drive out of their stances low and fast.

- Drill should progress from short-soft passes with high trajectories to passes more difficult to catch.

- Insist that all passes be caught with one hand and not trapped against the body.

- Emphasize the importance of concentrating on catching the football.

Safety Considerations:

- Proper warm-up should precede drill.
- Drill area (including sideline areas) should be clear of all foreign articles.
- Helmets should be worn with chinstraps snapped.
- Instruct returning pass receivers to stay clear of the drill area.

Variations:

- Can be used as a quarterback warm-up drill.
- Can be used as a tight end and running back drill.
- Can be used as a *distractor* drill by placing defensive backs on every yard stripe three yards from the sideline.

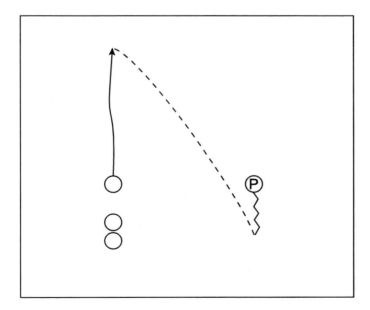

STATIONARY CONCENTRATION DRILL

Jerry L. Berndt
University of Missouri, Temple University, Rice University, University of Pennsylvania,
DePauw University, Dartmouth College
National Coach of the Year: Temple 1990

Objective: To teach and practice the proper fundamentals and techniques in catching the football under distracting conditions.

Equipment Needed: Footballs

Description:

- The coach should designate personnel as either defenders or receivers.

- Align the row of defenders (distracters) on a selected line of scrimmage.

- Position the row of receivers two yards away and perpendicular to the row of distracters (see diagram).

- The quarterback (coach) is positioned 15 yards in front of the row of receivers.

- On coach's command, the first defender aligns himself in a front-facing position to the first receiver.

- The quarterback passes the football to stationary receiver as defender grabs, pushes, pulls, shoves, and waves his arms in front of him.

- After the pass is completed or dropped, the receiver and defender change lines.

- The drill continues until all receivers have executed a sufficient number of distracting pass catches.

Coaching Points:

- Make sure receivers watch the football until it is secure in their hands.

- Instruct the receivers to catch the football with authority.

- Emphasize the importance of concentrating on catching the football.

Safety Considerations:

- Proper warm-up should precede this drill.

- Full equipment should be worn and chinstraps snapped during this drill.

- Distracters should be instructed not to hold the receivers.

- The coach should monitor closely the intensity of the drill.

Variations:

- Can be used with passes being thrown at varying heights and velocities.

- Can be used with receivers moving forward, backward, and laterally with defenders distracting them.

- Can be used as a tight end and running back drill.

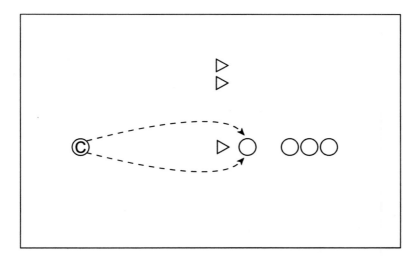

TWO-MAN TIP DRILL

Don W. Davis University of Texas at El Paso, West Texas State University

Objective: To teach and practice the proper fundamentals and techniques of catching a pass with special emphasis on concentration.

Equipment Needed: Footballs

Description:

- Align two rows of front-facing receivers five yards apart and perpendicular to two selected yard lines (see diagram).
- The coach, holding a football, is positioned 10 yards in front of the receivers.
- On command, the coach throws a soft pass to either receiver.
- In turn, the two receivers tip the ball back and forth as they run under control across the field.
- The two receivers try to execute ten tips each before they cross the drill area. Drill participants are instructed to alternate hands with each successful tip.
- Drill continues until all paired receivers have had a sufficient number of repetitions.

Coaching Points:

- Instruct the receivers to watch the flight of the football at all times.
- Make sure the receivers stop the forward most part of the football first as they tip the football back and forth.
- Emphasize the importance of concentrating on catching the football.

Safety Considerations:

- Proper warm-up should precede drill.
- The drill area (including sideline areas) should be clear of all foreign articles.
- Maintain a minimum distance of 10 yards between each pair of paired drill participants.

Variations:

- Can be used with football being tipped with one hand or both hands.
- Can be used with receivers changing directions after each tip.
- Can be used as a tight end or running back drill.

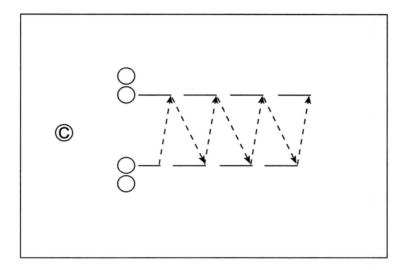

8

Option Offense Drills

OPTION DRILL

Steve Ayres
University of Richmond, Newberry College, Georgetown University,
East Tennessee State University, Wofford College
National Coach of the Year: Wofford 2002 and 2003

Objective: To teach and practice the proper fundamentals and techniques in the execution of the option from the double slot formation.

Equipment Needed: Footballs

Description:

- Position an option backfield (quarterback, fullback, two halfbacks [slot backs]) over a center on a selected line of scrimmage. The fullback is aligned two yards behind the quarterback (see diagram).

- The running back coach is positioned at the *read key* and the quarterback coach is positioned at the *pitch key*.

- Alternating backfields stand adjacent to the drill area and alternating quarterbacks can serve as centers.

- On quarterback's cadence and snap count, the offense executes the option as the *read key* and *pitch key* take their designated charges.

- If the *read key* steps up-field or steps *out*, the quarterback gives the football to the fullback who runs for the score. The quarterback continues to the *pitch key* with the *trailing* slot back.

- If the *read key* charges down the line, the quarterback *disconnects* from the fullback and goes to the *pitch key* as *fast* as he can. If the *pitch key* attacks the quarterback, the pitch is made immediately to the trailing slot back. If the *pitch key* does not *attack*, the quarterback attacks the inside shoulder of the *pitch key*, thus eliminating the *pitch key* from playing two phases of the option.

- The quarterback now executes the pitch to the trailing slot back.

- The drill continues until alternating backfields have had a sufficient number of repetitions to both the left and right and from various field positions.

Coaching Points:

- Always check to see that all backfield personnel are aligned correctly and are in their proper stances.

- Always stress the importance of proper execution.

- Insist that the drill be conducted at full speed.

- When the read key charges down the line, make sure the quarterbacks disconnect from the fullbacks, and as fast as he can, press the pitch key to make a decision.

- Instruct the slot back to always maintain the proper pitch relationship with the quarterback.

- Emphasize the importance of the fullback maintaining his running track on all option plays.

Safety Considerations:

- Proper warm-up should precede drill.

- The drill area should be clear of all foreign articles.

- It is imperative that the *read key* holds a hand shield in case of an accidental collision with the fullback.

Variation:

- Drill can be used with a variety of offensive formations.

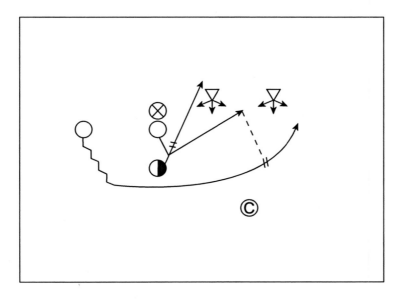

CUT AND READ*

Charles "Chuck" Broyles
University of Missouri-Rolla, Pittsburg State University
National Champions: Pittsburg State 1991
National Coach of the Year: 1991

Objective: To teach and practice the proper fundamentals and techniques in executing the inside handoff from the veer offense. Incorporated are skills related to running the correct mesh lane, receiving the handoff, making a full-speed north-south vertical cut for the running back, executing the inside-veer read and handoff, and accelerating to the pitch key for the quarterback.

Equipment Needed: Five large rubber trashcans, a hand shield, and footballs

Description:

- Position four rubber trashcans in a rectangular pattern approximately two- yards wide and three-yards deep adjacent to a selected line of scrimmage. A fifth trashcan is placed in the center of the rectangle (see diagram).

- Align a quarterback directly behind one of the front trashcans.

- Align a running back in his normal position, four-yards deep and head-up the center trashcan.

- Other drill participants stand behind the drill area.

- Position a coach, holding a hand shield, behind the center trashcan and another coach behind the opposite front trashcan.

- On his cadence and snap count, the quarterback moves to the veer mesh point with the running back. At the same time, the quarterback looks for a hand signal from the coach stepping from behind the opposite front trashcan. If he holds up one finger, the quarterback hands off to the running back. If he holds up two fingers, the quarterback will ride the running back, pull the football and accelerate to the pitch key while calling out the number of fingers held up by the coach.

- If the handoff is executed, the running back will react to the coach who is stepping from behind the middle trashcan by cutting in the opposite direction and sprinting through and past the two back trashcans.

- The drill continues until all the quarterbacks and running backs have had a sufficient number of repetitions from both left- and right-offensive alignments.

*Reprinted with permission from 101 Winning Football Drills: From the Legends of the Game by Jerry Tolley

Coaching Points:

- Always check to see that the quarterbacks and running backs are aligned correctly and are in their proper stances.

- Stress the importance of proper executions.

- Insist that the drill be conducted at full speed.

- Make sure all the quarterbacks use the proper inside-veer footwork, reads and calls out the number signaled by the coach as they accelerate out of the handoff and to the pitch key.

- Make sure the running backs run their proper inside-veer path, form the proper handoff pocket, react correctly to the coach's stepping from behind the middle trashcan, and accelerate through and pass the back two trashcans.

- Instruct the running backs to use a *soft squeeze* on the football as they drive through the mesh point.

Safety Considerations:

- Proper warm-up should precede the drill.

- It is imperative that the coach standing behind the middle trashcan holds a hand shield in case of an accidental collision with the running back.

Variation:

- Can incorporate a third defender holding up a hand shield two-yards behind the rear trashcans and have the running back execute various moves such as a 360-degree spin or side step.

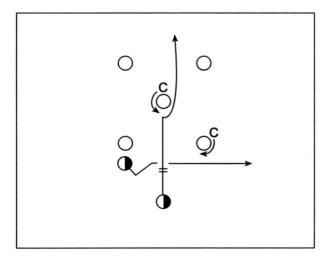

ARC DRILL

Bruce C. Arians
Virginia Polytechnic Institute and State University, Mississippi State University, University of Alabama, Temple University, Kansas City Chiefs, New Orleans Saints, Indianapolis Colts, Cleveland Browns

Objective: To teach and practice the proper fundamentals and techniques of executing the arc block on a defensive back.

Equipment Needed: Large blocking shield

Description:

- Position a defensive back, holding a large blocking shield, in his normal alignment.
- A tight end is positioned on a selected line of scrimmage in a proper arc block relationship to the defensive back (see diagram).
- Other tight ends stand in line behind the first tight end.
- The coach is positioned five yards behind the defensive back.
- On coach's cadence and snap count, the tight end drives from his stance and executes an arc block on the defensive back—who is attacking the line of scrimmage.
- Drill continues until all tight ends have had a sufficient number of repetitions.
- Drill should be conducted from both left and right formations and from various field positions.

Coaching Points:

- Always check to see that tight ends are aligned correctly and are in their proper stances.
- Instruct the tight ends to establish their blocking path by taking three steps parallel to the line of scrimmage and then focus on a *blocking junction* 17 yards from the football.
- Make sure the tight ends keep their heads up with eyes forward on the defender until the block is executed.
- Insist that all tight ends use the proper fundamentals and techniques in executing the *arc* block.

Safety Considerations:

- Proper warm-up should precede drill.

- Drill area should be clear of all foreign articles.

- Instruct all tight ends as to the proper fundamentals and techniques of executing the *arc* block.

- The drill should progress from half speed to full speed.

- The coach should monitor closely the intensity of the drill.

- Instruct the defensive back not to *jam* the blocker in the head area.

Variations:

- Can vary the position of the defensive back.

- Can be used as a form or live blocking drill.

- Can be used as a running back blocking drill with the running back blocking on the defensive end or defensive back.

- Can be used as a defensive back drill.

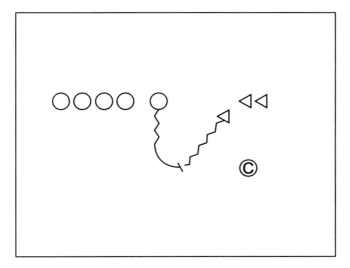

BOARD DRILL

Carlton E. "Pete" Stout
Catawba College

Objective: To teach and practice the proper fundamentals and techniques in the execution of the triple option from the wishbone formation. Special emphasis is placed on huddle discipline and break, alignment, stance, explosion off the ball, and the execution of the pitch.

Equipment Needed: Seven boards (8' x 10" x 2"), seven blocking shields, one large blocking dummy, and footballs

Description:

- Lay seven boards four feet apart and perpendicular to a selected line of scrimmage.

- Align a defender holding a blocking shield in a straddle position over each board.

- A single defender with a large blocking dummy is placed on the line of scrimmage 10 yards outside the board area (see diagram).

- A defensive end is positioned in his normal alignment and is instructed to defend the two-way option.

- The complete offensive team breaks the huddle and takes its positions over the football in a two-tight end wishbone formation.

- Other offensive units are positioned behind the first offense.

- On quarterback's cadence and ball snap, the offense runs the triple option with the offensive line firing out and executing drive blocks on the shield holders. The lead back executes a *kick-out* block on the outside blocking dummy.

- The quarterback is instructed always to fake the ball to the fullback. After the fake, he either keeps or pitches the ball to the running back depending on the charge of the defensive end.

- Drill continues until alternating offenses have had a sufficient number of repetitions.

- Drill should be conducted both left and right.

Coaching Points:

- Always check to see that all personnel are aligned correctly and are in their proper stances.

- Insist on good huddle discipline and break.

- Emphasize the importance of everyone driving off the football together.

- Instruct the quarterback always to fake to the fullback and then to execute the two-way option.

Safety Considerations:

- Proper warm-up should precede drill.

- All boards should be beveled and checked for splinters daily.

- The dummy holder should be instructed to release his dummy as the *kick-out* block is being executed.

- Instruct all linemen as to the proper fundamentals and techniques of the shoulder block.

Variations:

- Can be used with a variety of option formations.

- Can be used with a load-blocking scheme with the lead blocker.

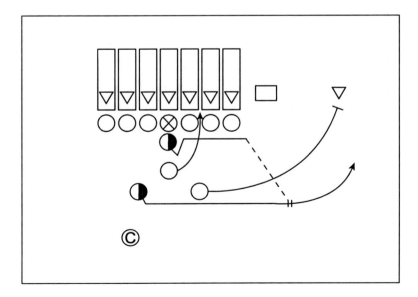

PLAY PERFECTION – WIDENER'S DREAM PLAY*

<table>
<tr><td>

William B. "Bill" Manlove, Jr.
Lafayette College, University of Delaware, Widener University,
Delaware Valley College, La Salle University
National Champions: Widener 1977 and 1981
National Coach of the Year: Widener 1977 and 1981
AFCA President: 1991

</td></tr>
</table>

Objective: To teach and practice the proper fundamentals in the execution of Widener's Dream Play—the outside veer. Incorporated are skills related to the center-quarterback ball exchange, blocking, and ballhandling.

Equipment Needed: Line-spacing strip, six hand shields, and footballs

Description:

- Place a line-spacing strip at the midpoint of a selected line of scrimmage.

- Position a noseguard, tackle, end, linebacker, strong safety, and cornerback in their normal positions. All defenders are holding hand shields.

- The offensive personnel (center, slot-side guard, tackle, split end, slot-back, quarterback, and running backs) break from the huddle and take their positions over the football.

- Other offensive personnel stand behind performing offensive players or serve as defensive players.

- On the quarterback's cadence and ball snap, the offense executes the outside veer as the defense reacts to the play.

- The drill continues until alternating offensives have had a sufficient number of repetitions.

- The drill should be conducted from both left and right formations and from various field positions.

Coaching Points:

- Always check to see that all personnel are aligned correctly and are in their proper stances.

- Make sure that center-quarterback exchange is executed property.

*Reprinted with permission from *101 Winning Football Drills: From the Legends of the Game* by Jerry Tolley

- Emphasize the importance of the entire offense driving off the ball as a unit.

- Instruct dive backs that it is imperative to run the dive lane hard and fast.

- Insist that all the defenders react to and give good resistance to blockers.

- The coach should signal the defensive end to close on the dive back, take the quarterback, or play pitch before each play.

- All coaching corrections should be made on the run and should not interfere with the tempo of the drill.

Safety Considerations:

- Proper warm-up should precede the drill.

- The drill area should be clear of all foreign articles.

- The drill should progress from formwork to live work.

- The coach should monitor closely the intensity of the drill.

- Instruct the defensive end not to be overly aggressive.

- When the drill is conducted live, the training staff should be placed on special alert.

Variations:

- Can be used as a form or live drill.

- Can be used with certain players designated as live performers such as the defensive end.

- Can be run to the tight end side.

- Can be used as a defensive drill.

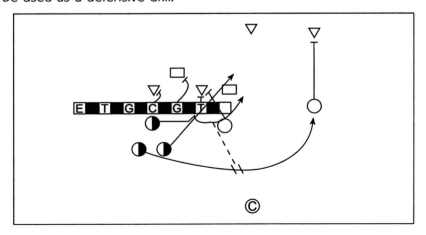

INSIDE-OUTSIDE OPTION DRILL

Kenneth J. Matous
Wichita State University, East Carolina University, University of Cincinnati,
Austin Peay State University, Western Carolina University,
Carolina Cobras, Tulsa Talons

Objective: To teach and practice the proper fundamentals and techniques in the execution of the option from the I formation. Incorporated are skills of reading, ball handling, and blocking.

Equipment Needed: Footballs

Description:

- Position a defensive end, a strong safety, and a cornerback in their normal alignments across from a selected line of scrimmage.

- The coach, with a football in hand, stands at the defensive tackle position.

- The offensive personnel (center, quarterback, fullback, tailback, tight end, and flanker) break the huddle and take their positions over the football.

- Other offensive personnel stand behind the performing offensive players.

- On quarterback's cadence and ball snap, the offense executes the triple option as the defenders react to the play.

- The quarterback moves down the line executing the handoff to the fullback. After the handoff is completed, the coach immediately pitches the quarterback another football.

- The quarterback uses the second football to option the defensive end. According to the defensive end's charge, the quarterback either keeps the football and cuts upfield or pitches the football to the tailback that is running his option path.

- The tight end and flanker execute the *arc* block and *stalk* block respectively.

- Drill continues until alternating offensive personnel have had a sufficient number of repetitions.

- Drill should be conducted from both left and right formations and from various field positions.

Coaching Points:

- Always check to see that all personnel are aligned correctly and are in their proper stances.

- Stress the importance of proper execution.
- Make sure the quarterback uses the instructed techniques in riding the fullback and optioning the defensive end.
- Insist that the flanker and tight end execute their blocks correctly.
- Instruct the defensive end to either hard-charge the quarterback, take the pitch, or slow-play the quarterback.
- Encourage all defensive personnel to react with enthusiasm to each play.
- Insist that the drill be conducted at full speed.

Safety Considerations:
- Proper warm-up should precede drill.
- Drill area should be clear of all foreign articles.
- Drill should progress from form work to *brisk* work.
- The coach should monitor closely the intensity of the drill.
- Instruct the defensive end not to be over-aggressive.

Variations:
- Can be used to attack the split end side of the formation.
- Can be used with varying defensive coverages.
- Can incorporate the veer pass.
- Can be used as a defensive drill.

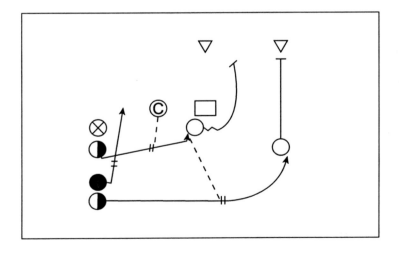

TRIPLE-OPTION KEY DRILL*

| **William F. "Bill" Yeoman** |
| United States Military Academy, University of Michigan, University of Houston |
| College Football Hall of Fame: 2001 |

Objective: To teach and practice the proper fundamentals and techniques in the execution of the three-way option. Incorporated are skills of reading for the quarterbacks, running the correct *mesh* lane, and taking the handoff and pitch for the running backs.

Equipment Needed: Line-spacing strip, a hand shield, and footballs

Description:

- Place a line-spacing strip at the midpoint of a selected line of scrimmage.

- The coach, holding a hand shield, is positioned at either the defensive 4 or 5 technique.

- Alternating quarterbacks are placed at the 9 technique.

- The coach and the defensive end (quarterback) coordinate their defensive charge. (Coach and end slant in, coach and end slant out, and coach slants in and end slants out.)

- The offensive personnel (center, quarterback, fullback, and running backs) break the huddle and take their positions over the football.

- Other offensive backfields are positioned behind the performing offensive players.

- On the cadence and ball snap, the offense executes the three-way option as the defenders make their designated charges.

- The drill continues until the alternating backfields have had a sufficient number of repetitions.

- The drill should be conducted from both left and right formations and from various field positions.

Coaching Points:

- Always check to see that all personnel are aligned correctly and are in their proper stances.

*Reprinted with permission from *101 Winning Football Drills: From the Legends of the Game* by Jerry Tolley

- Instruct the defenders to execute their charges quickly and in a well-defined manner.

- Stress the importance of proper execution.

- Make sure the quarterbacks use the instructed techniques in executing the handoffs and pitches.

- After and only after quarterbacks have become comfortable with their reads, instruct defenders to play a little more *cat and mouse* with their charges.

- Insist that the drill be conducted at full speed.

- The coach should designate defensive charges that allow different quarterbacks to work on their particular weaknesses such as the handoff, quarterback keep, or pitch.

Safety Considerations:

- Proper warm-up should precede the drill.

- The drill area should be clear of all foreign articles.

- It is imperative that the coach, standing at the 4 or 5 technique, holds a hand shield in case of a collision with the dive back.

Variations:

- Can use with the two-way option (outside veer) by moving the coach to the 9 technique and other defender to the strong safety position.

- Can be used in attacking the split end side.

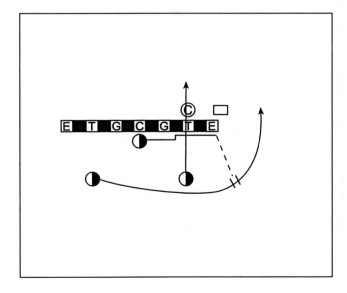

OPTION DRILL

Jack S. Bicknell
University of Maine, Boston College, Barcelona Dragons, Scotland Claymores
World Bowl Champions: Barcelona 1997

Objectives: To teach and practice the proper fundamentals and techniques in the execution of the option from an I formation. Incorporated are skills related to footwork, ball handling, reading, hand-eye coordination, and pitch for quarterbacks; and footwork, ball handling, and receiving a handoff or pitch for running backs.

Equipment Needed: Line-spacing strip and footballs

Description:

- Place a line-spacing strip at the midpoint of a selected line of scrimmage.

- The coach, with a football in hand, is aligned at the defensive end position.

- The offensive personnel (center, quarterback, fullback, and tailback) break the huddle and take their positions over the football.

- Other offensive backfields stand behind the performing offense.

- On quarterback's cadence and ball snap, the offense executes either the trap or dive option toward the defensive end (coach) as shown in diagram. The quarterback is instructed always to give the football to the first back.

- After the handoff is executed, the coach pitches his football to the quarterback.

- The quarterback, with second football in hand, options the defensive end (coach) and either cuts upfield or pitches the football to the tailback.

- Drill continues until alternating backfields have had a sufficient number of repetitions.

- Drill should be conducted from both left and right formations and from various field positions.

Coaching Points:

- Always check to see that all personnel are aligned correctly and are in their proper stances.

- Stress the importance of proper execution.

- Instruct the quarterbacks to get their heads around quickly after the handoff is executed.

- The coach should vary the speed and trajectory of his pitches to the quarterbacks.
- Insist that the drill be conducted at full speed.

Safety Considerations:

- Proper warm-up should precede drill.
- Drill area should be clear of all foreign articles.

Variation:

- Can be used with a variety of option formations.

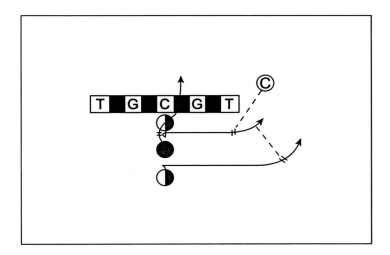

RIDE AND DECIDE*

Fisher DeBerry

Wofford College, Appalachian State University, United States Air Force Academy
National Coach of the Year: Air Force 1985
Fellowship of Christian Athletes Grant Teaff Coach of the Year: 1998
AFCA President: 1996

Objective: To teach and practice the proper fundamental and techniques in the execution of the triple-option versus a seven-man front. Special emphasis is placed on the quarterback making his first and second read under pressure.

Equipment Needed: Football

Description:

- Align a defensive tackle and a defensive end in their normal seven-man front alignment on a selected line of scrimmage.

- Position a quarterback, a fullback, and a pitch back in their normal triple-option alignment over the defense.

- Alternating offensive backfields stand behind the performing offensive players.

- On the quarterback's cadence and snap count, the backfield executes the triple-option as defenders execute a variety of designated charges.

- If the defensive tackle and the defensive end both run a *hot stunt* (see diagram A), the quarterback should pull the football, take a drop step, stop and pitch the football to the pitch back.

- If the defensive tackle closes on the fullback and the defensive end slow plays the quarterback, the quarterback should pull the football and attack the defensive end by dipping the shoulders to the inside to draw his tackle. The quarterback then pitches the football to the pitch back (see diagram B).

- If the defensive tackle drives up the field to take the quarterback, the quarterback should hand the football to the fullback (see diagram C).

- The drill continues until all the backfield personnel have had a sufficient number of repetitions from both left and right formations and from various field positions.

*Reprinted with permission from 101 Winning Football Drills: From the Legends of the Game by Jerry Tolley

Coaching Points:

- Always check to see that the backfield personnel are aligned correctly and are in their proper stances.

- Stress the importance of proper execution.

- Insist that the drill be conducted at full speed.

- Instruct the backfield personnel to always take their designated option paths.

Safety Considerations:

- Proper warm-up should precede the drill.

- The drill area should be clear of all foreign articles.

- The drill should progress from formwork to full speed.

- The coach should monitor closely the intensity of the drill.

Variation:

- Can be used in executing the triple option against an eight-man front.

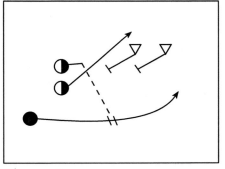

Diagram A

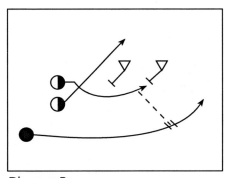

Diagram B

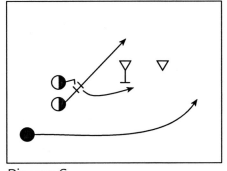

Diagram C

OPTION DRILL

Rick E. Carter (Deceased)
Earlham College, Hanover College, University of Dayton, College of the Holy Cross
National Champions: Dayton 1980
National Coach of the Year: Dayton 1980
National Coach of the Year: Holy Cross 1983

Objective: To teach and practice the proper fundamentals and techniques in the execution of the option into the sideline from the I formation.

Equipment Needed: One cone and footballs

Description:

- Align an offense (center, quarterback, fullback, and tailback) over the football on either hash mark on a selected line of scrimmage.

- Other offensive backfields stand behind the performing offensive players.

- Position a defensive end in his normal position on the hash mark side of the field.

- A cone is placed at the outside leg alignment of an imaginary play-side offensive tackle.

- On cadence and ball snap, the quarterback fakes to the fullback and then options the defensive end that is reacting to the play. The quarterback either keeps the football and cuts upfield, or pitches it to the tailback depending of the charge of the defensive end.

- The object of the drill is for the quarterback or tailback to gain five yards without being touched by the defensive end (one hand on the tailback and two hands on the quarterback constitute a successful touch).

- Drill continues until alternating backfields have had a sufficient number of repetitions.

- Drill should be conducted to both the strong and weak sides of the formation and from both hash marks.

Coaching Points:

- Always check to see that backfield personnel are aligned correctly and are in their proper stances.

- Stress the importance of proper execution.

- Instruct the quarterbacks to look through the dive fake to the defensive end.
- Instruct the defensive end to use either a *crash* or *feather* technique in playing the quarterback.
- If the quarterback keeps the football, he must run outside the cone marker.
- Make sure the tailback stays on his option path.
- Insist that the drill be conducted at full speed.

Safety Considerations:

- Proper warm-up should precede drill.
- The drill area (including sideline areas) should be clear of all foreign articles.
- Instruct the defensive end to wait two counts if he uses the *crash* technique.
- This drill is not recommended as a contact drill.

Variations:

- Can be used with a variety of option formations.
- Can keep score by awarding points for successful offensive and defensive plays (one point for the offense if either the quarterback or tailback gains five yards and two points for the defense for successful touches; the defense is also awarded two points for every faulty pitch by the quarterback).
- Can be used as a defensive end drill.

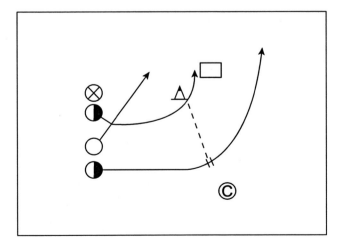

TRIPLE OPTION*

Frank Solich
University of Nebraska, Ohio University

Objective: To teach and practice the proper fundamentals and technique in executing the triple option from the I formation.

Equipment Needed: Line spacing strip, a hand shield, and footballs

Description:

- Place a line-spacing strip at the midpoint of a selected line of scrimmage.

- Align a backfield in the proper triple-option I formation behind the line-spacing strip.

- Position the running back coach, holding a hand shield, at the defensive tackle position and the quarterback coach at the defensive end position.

- Other offensive backfields stand behind the performing offensive backfield.

- On the quarterback's cadence and snap count, the I-formation backfield executes the triple option as the defenders (coaches) execute their designated charges.

- If the defensive tackle (coach) closes on the fullback, the quarterback pulls the football and proceeds to the pitch read. If the defensive tackle (coach) maintains his width, the quarterback hands the football to the fullback.

- If the defensive end (quarterbacks coach) closes on the quarterback, he pitches the football to the I back. If the defensive end (coach) maintains his width, the quarterback keeps the football and sprints up the field.

- The drill continues until the I-back personnel have had a sufficient number of repetitions from both the left and right formations and from various field alignments.

Coaching Points:

- Always check to see that the I backfields are aligned correctly and that all the drill participants are in their proper stances.

- Stress the importance of proper execution.

- Insist that the drill be conducted at full speed.

- Instruct all the backfield personnel as to their designated option paths.

*Reprinted with permission from *101 Winning Football Drills: From the Legends of the Game* by Jerry Tolley

- The coach should monitor closely the quarterbacks' read and handoff in the mesh lane and the I backs' pitch relationship with the quarterbacks.

- Instruct the quarterbacks to take a 45-degree angle step and extend the football back toward the fullback while he reads the charges of the defensive tackle and defensive end to determine if he should hand off to the fullbacks or pull the football and execute his second option.

- In reading the dive, the quarterbacks should place the ball in the fullbacks' pocket at the numbers and ride the fullback as they read the defensive tackle.

- Instruct the I backs to read the charge of the defensive end, and if the end attacks the quarterback, they should *throttle down* so they can maintain the proper pitch relationship with the quarterback.

- Instruct the quarterbacks that if the defensive tackle closes and the defensive end slow plays the pitch, the quarterback must pull the football from the fullback and attack the defensive end as the second option is executed.

Safety Considerations:

- Proper warm-up should precede the drill.

- The drill area should be clear of all foreign articles.

- It is imperative that the coach aligned at the dive read holds a hand shield in case of an accidental collision with the fullback.

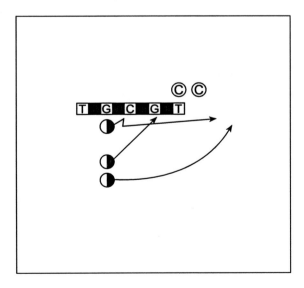

OPTION DRILL

George F. "Buddy" Sasser
Appalachian State University, Wofford College, East Tennessee State University

Objective: To teach and practice the proper fundamentals and techniques in the execution of the triple option from a wishbone formation. Incorporated are skills of reading, faking, and pitching the football for the quarterbacks; running the correct mesh lane, faking, blocking, and receiving the pitch for the backs; and blocking for the wide receiver.

Equipment Needed: Two hand shields, one large blocking dummy, and footballs

Description:

- Position a defensive tackle, an end, a strong safety and a cornerback in their normal alignments across from a selected line of scrimmage. The tackle and cornerbacks hold hand shields and the strong safety holds a large blocking dummy. The defensive end does not have a dummy.

- The offensive personnel (center, quarterback, fullback, tailback, and wide receiver) break the huddle and take their positions over the football.

- Alternating drill participants stand adjacent to drill area or can serve as defenders.

- On quarterback's cadence and ball snap, the offense executes the triple option as the defenders react with pre-designated charges.

- Drill continues until alternating offenses have had a sufficient number of repetitions.

- Drill should be conducted from both left and right formations and from various field positions.

Coaching Points:

- Always check to see that all personnel are aligned correctly and are in their proper stances.

- Make sure all offensive players execute their assignments correctly.

- The coach should monitor closely the *reads* of the quarterback.

- Insist that all defenders react to the play at full speed.

Safety Considerations:

- Proper warm-up should precede drill.
- Drill area should be clear of all foreign articles.
- Drill should progress from brisk blocking to live blocking.
- The coach should monitor closely the intensity of the drill.

Variations:

- Can be used with a variety of option formations.
- Can be used as a *brisk* blocking or live blocking drill.
- Can designate one defensive man at a time to be live.
- Can be used as a defensive drill.

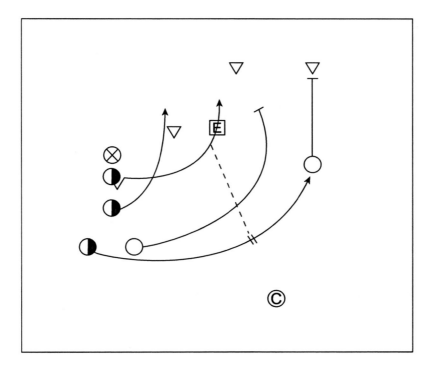

TAPE*

Kenneth "Ken" Sparks
Tennesse Technological University, Carson-Newman College
National Champions: Carson-Newman 1983, 1984, 1986, 1988, and 1989
National Coach of the Year: Carson-Newman 1984
Fellowship of Christian Athletes Grant Teaff Coach of the Year: 1999

Objective: To teach and practice the proper fundamentals and techniques in executing the inside handoff from the veer offense. Incorporated are skills related to running the correct veer lane for the running backs and reading the *no-mesh* option for the quarterbacks.

Equipment Needed: One large block dummy, a hand shield, and footballs

Description:

- Align a veer backfield on a selected line of scrimmage.

- Place a large block dummy behind the line of scrimmage and at a 45-degree angle adjacent to the quarterback (see diagram).

- Align two coaches, one holding a hand shield at the dive read position and the other at the pitch read position. A player or manager is aligned at the offensive tackle position.

- Other drill participants stand behind the performing offensive players.

- On his cadence and snap count, the quarterback steps into the line of scrimmage avoiding the block dummy and points the football at the dive-read defender (coach).

- The running back drives to the outside leg of the offensive guard and *brushes* the tail of the offensive tackle (player or manager) that is blocking down to the inside.

- The quarterback reads the dive defender's (coach's) charge and either hand the football to the running back or proceeds to and executes the pitch read against the pitch defender (coach).

- The drill continues until all the drill participants have had a sufficient number of repetitions from both left and right formations.

---

*Reprinted with permission from *101 Winning Football Drills: From the Legends of the Game* by Jerry Tolley

Coaching Points:

- Always check to see that all the drill participants are aligned correctly and are in their proper stances.

- Stress the importance of proper execution.

- Insist that the drill be conducted at full speed.

- Instruct the dive-and-pitch defenders to present the quarterbacks with various reads.

- Instruct the quarterbacks to always point the football at the dive read defender, and if the dive read defender comes to take the football, he should pull the football and proceed to the pitch read.

- Instruct the pitch back to always maintain the proper pitch relationship to the quarterback.

Safety Considerations:

- Proper warm-up should precede the drill.

- The drill area should be clear of all foreign articles.

- It is imperative that the coach positioned at the dive read hold a hand shield in case of an accidental collision with the dive back.

Variation:

- Can be used in the execution of the two-way option, the counter option, and the mid-line option.

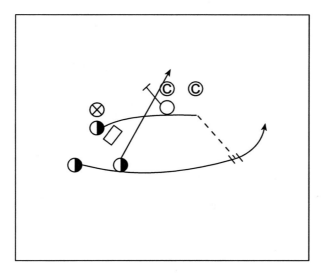

QUARTERBACK OPTION DRILL

Scotty Glacken
Georgetown University

Objective: To teach and practice the proper fundamentals and techniques in the execution of the pitch on the option. Incorporated are skills related to footwork and reading.

Equipment Needed: Three large blocking dummies, one hand shield, and footballs

Description:

- Lay two large blocking dummies perpendicular to a selected line of scrimmage at the defensive tackle and end positions. A third dummy is placed upright in the offensive backfield one yard in front of the defensive end position (see diagram).

- A defensive end with a hand shield is aligned in his normal position. He is instructed to charge the quarterback, charge the halfback, or *string pressure* the quarterback.

- The center, quarterback and pitch halfback break the huddle and take their positions over the football.

- Other drill participants stand adjacent to drill area.

- On cadence and ball snap, the quarterback moves down the line simulating a handoff and then executes the option with the end.

- The quarterback (depending on the charge of the defensive end) either keeps the football and cuts upfield between the two dummies, or pitches the football to the halfback who is running his option path.

- Drill continues until all personnel have had a sufficient number of repetitions.

- Drill should be conducted both left and right and from various field positions.

Coaching Points:

- Always check to see that backfield personnel are aligned correctly and are in proper stances.

- Stress the importance of proper execution.

- Instruct the quarterbacks to work for an inside hip position on the defensive end.

- Instruct the tailbacks to run the proper option path.

- Insist that the drill be conducted at full speed.

Safety Considerations:

- Proper warm-up should precede drill.

- The coach should instruct defensive end not to be over-aggressive when charging the quarterback.

Variations:

- Can be used to simulate triple option, pure option, and reverse option.

- Can be used as a defensive end drill.

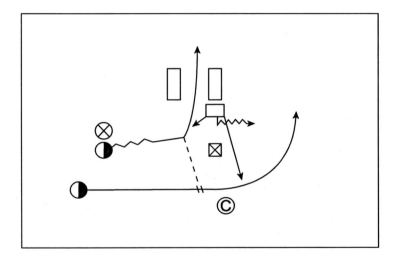

QUARTERBACK OPTION RUNNING DRILL

Clayton E. Johnson
Elon University, Newberry College

Objective: To teach and practice the proper fundamentals and techniques of reading and reacting in the execution of the outside option. Incorporated are skills related to agility, quickness, and the development of peripheral vision.

Equipment Needed: Three large blocking dummies and footballs

Description:

- Position a center and quarterback over the football at the midpoint of a selected line of scrimmage.
- Lay three large blocking dummies perpendicular to the neutral zone at the defensive guard, tackle, and end positions (see diagram).
- A defensive tackle and an end are positioned head up to the two outside dummies.
- Alternating quarterbacks stand adjacent to the drill area.
- The coach stands four yards outside the defensive end and parallel to the quarterback. From this position he signals the two defenders as to their defensive charge (one finger – tackle and end slant out; two fingers – tackle and end slant in; three fingers – tackle slants in and the end slants out).
- On cadence and ball snap, the quarterback moves down the line making his *pitch read* as the defenders make their instructed charges.
- Drill continues until all quarterbacks have had a sufficient number of repetitions.
- Drill should be conducted both left and right and from various field positions.

Coaching Points:

- Always check to see that quarterbacks are in their proper stances.
- Make sure all quarterbacks take the desired angle down the line of scrimmage.
- Always check to see that the quarterbacks read and react correctly according to the charge of the defenders.
- Instruct the quarterbacks to turn upfield immediately if the defensive tackle should penetrate the outside gap.
- Insist that the drill be conducted at full speed.

Safety Considerations:

- Proper warm-up should precede drill.

- Under no circumstances should this a contact drill.

Variation:

- Can incorporate running backs.

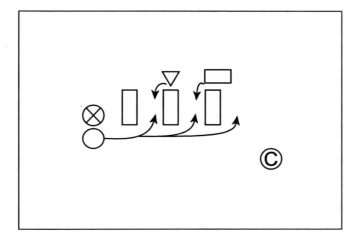

READING AND OPTIONING DRILL

Al P. Kincaid
East Carolina University, University of Wyoming, Orlando Renegades,
University of Alabama, Arkansas State University,
University of North Alabama, Temple University

Objective: To teach and practice the proper fundamentals and techniques in the execution of the triple option from a wishbone formation.

Equipment Needed: Line-spacing strip and footballs

Description:

• Place a line-spacing strip at the midpoint of a selected line of scrimmage.

• A defensive tackle (read man) is placed over the offensive tackle position.

• The coach, holding a football, stands at the 9 technique.

• The offensive personnel (center, quarterback, fullback, and off-side halfback) break the huddle and take their positions over the football.

• Other offensive backfields stand behind the performing offensive players.

• On coach's instructions, the defensive tackle and 9 technique (coach) coordinate their defensive charge.

• On cadence and ball snap, the offense executes the triple option as the defensive tackle makes his designated charge

• If the quarterback hands the ball to the fullback, the 9 technique (coach) immediately pitches the quarterback the football he is holding.

• The quarterback catches the football pitched to him by the (coach) and depending on the charge of the 9 technique, either cuts upfield or pitches the football to the running back who is running his option path.

• If the quarterback does not hand the football off to the fullback, the coach does not pitch him the second ball and the previous description is repeated.

• Drill continues until alternating backfields have run a sufficient number of repetitions.

• Drill should be conducted both left and right and from various field positions.

Coaching Points:

- Always check to see that offensive backs are aligned correctly and are in their proper stances.

- Make sure all quarterbacks take the desired angle down the line of scrimmage.

- Instruct quarterbacks always to watch the defender who is being optioned.

- Make sure the quarterbacks catch the football pitched by the coach before the final option executed.

- Instruct fullbacks and tailbacks to run their correct option paths.

Safety Considerations:

- Proper warm-up should precede drill.

- Drill area should be clear of all foreign articles.

- The coach should not pitch the football to the quarterback too hard.

Variations:

- Can be used without the second football.

- Can be used with tackle and 9 technique (coach) executing various defensive charges (double slant in, double slant out, cross charge, etc.).

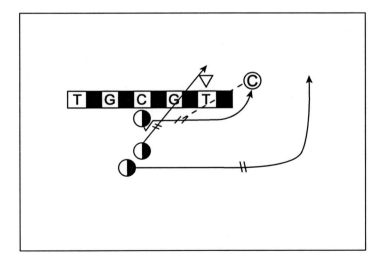

VEER READ DRILL

Joe R. Morrison (Deceased)
University of Chattanooga, University of New Mexico, University of South Carolina
National Coach of the Year: South Carolina 1984

Objective: To teach and practice the proper fundamentals and techniques in the execution of the veer offense. Incorporated are skills related to footwork and reading for the quarterback and running the correct veer path and footwork for the running backs.

Equipment Needed: Six cones, four hand shields, and footballs

Description:

- Align cones on each side of the center at distances that represent the proper alignment of the offensive guards, tackles, and ends.

- A defensive tackle and end, holding hand shields, are aligned in their normal positions (see diagram).

- The offensive personnel (center, quarterback, and running backs) break the huddle and take their regular positions over the football.

- Alternating offensive backfields are positioned behind the performing offensive players.

- The coach stands behind the offense and signals a coordinated charge for the defenders.

- On cadence and ball snap, the offense executes the veer option as the defenders react and makes their designated charges.

- Drill continues until alternating backfields have had a sufficient number of repetitions.

- Drill should be conducted from both left and right formations and from various field positions.

Coaching Points:

- Always check to see that all backfield personnel are aligned correctly and are in their proper stances.

- Stress the importance of proper execution.

- Make sure all quarterbacks execute their reads correctly and turn and sprint up the field 10 yards on both quarterback keeps and pitch options.

- Instruct the dive backs to form a good handoff pocket and to stay on their veer paths.

- Instruct the pitch backs to stay on their option path and to sprint 10 yards downfield on each play.

- Insist that the drill be conducted at full speed.

Safety Considerations:

- Proper warm-up should precede drill.

- Drill area should be clear of all foreign articles.

- The drill should progress from form work to full speed.

- The coach should monitor closely the intensity of the drill.

Variations:

- Can be used to teach and practice the outside veer.

- Can incorporate tight ends, wide receivers, and defensive backs.

- Can be used as a defensive drill.

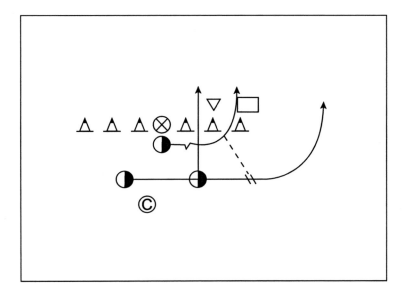

OPTION DRILL*

Roy Lee Kidd
Eastern Kentucky University, Morehead State University
National Champions: Eastern Kentucky 1979 and 1982
National Coach of the Year: Eastern Kentucky 1980 and 1981
College Football Hall of Fame: 2003
AFCA President: 1998

Objective: To teach and practice the proper fundamentals and techniques in executing the handoff and pitch on the option play from the I formation.

Equipment Needed: Line-spacing strip, four cones, and footballs

Description:

- Place a line-spacing strip at the midpoint of a selected line of scrimmage.

- Cones are positioned on the line of scrimmage 10-yards outside the line-spacing strip. Additional cones are placed seven-yards downfield just inside each hash mark.

- Align a defensive end in his normal position.

- Position two quarterbacks side by side under centers at designated points on the line-spacing strip (see diagram). Three yards should separate the paired quarterbacks.

- A fullback and a tailback take an I-formation alignment relationship to the paired quarterback. (Tailback to the playside and fullback to the backside as shown in diagram.)

- Other offensive personnel stand behind the performing offensive players.

- On the backside quarterback's cadence, the centers snap the footballs. The backside quarterback executes a handoff to the fullback and continues down the line of scrimmage with his fake.

- The playside quarterback fakes to an imaginary fullback and then options the defensive end as he reacts to the play. The quarterback now pitches the football to the tailback or cuts and sprints upfield. The two cones, placed 10-yards outside the line-spacing strip, are used as an aiming point for the tailback's option course.

- Quarterbacks should alternate between backside and playside alignments.

*Reprinted with permission from *101 Winning Football Drills: From the Legends of the Game* by Jerry Tolley

- The drill continues until the alternating backfield has had a sufficient number of repetitions.
- The drill should be conducted from both left and right formations and from various field positions.

Coaching Points:

- Always check to see that all personnel are aligned correctly and are in their proper stances.
- Stress the importance of proper execution.
- Insist that the drill participants, with the exception of backside quarterbacks, sprint past the cones placed seven yards downfield.

Safety Considerations:

- Proper warm-up should precede the drill.
- The drill area should be clear of all foreign articles.
- Maintain a minimum distance of three yards between paired quarterbacks.

Variations:

- Can be used with a variety of option formations.
- Can incorporate other offensive and defensive personnel.

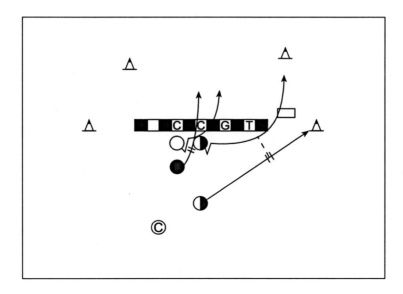

HOOK-UP DRILLS

Paul Johnson
University of Hawaii, Georgia Southern University, United States Naval Academy
National Champions: Georgia Southern 1999 and 2000
National Coach of the Year: Georgia Southern 1997, 1998, 1999, and 2000

Objective: To teach and practice the proper fundamentals and techniques in the execution of the handoff between the quarterback and fullback on the triple option. The drill is conducted in three phases.

Equipment Needed: Footballs

Description:

Phase I: The *blind set* phase is designed to help the quarterback and fullback get a *feel* for delivering and receiving the handoff on the triple option by working on the first two and three steps of the play.

- Align a quarterback under a center on a designated line of scrimmage.

- Align a fullback in a sprinter's stance five yards from the tip of the football.

- Other drill participants stand adjacent to the drill area.

- On quarterback's cadence and snap count, the quarterback receives the snap, takes his first two steps, and extends the football back towards the fullback.

- Also on the snap count, the fullback runs the first three steps of his running path.

- The coach stands adjacent to the drill area and observes and critiques the mechanics of all movements.

- This phase of the drill continues until all drill participants have had a sufficient number of repetitions.

- Drill should be conducted both left and right.

Phase II: The *fit* phase of the drill begins at the ending point of the *blind set* phase of the drill and is designed to help the quarterback and fullback get the *feel* of the handoff.

- The center, quarterback, and fullback are aligned as noted in Phase I.

- During the *fit* phase, a defender (coach or extra player) is placed at the *read key* position and makes the designated charges.

- The quarterback now *squeezes* the football while checking his hand placement on the football as he executes the handoff.

- The fullback also *squeezes* the football and checks his hand pressure as his arms are folded over the football.

- The quarterback continues to carry out his option techniques and either makes the handoff or pulls the football based on his *read key's* charge.

- On coach's whistle the fullback continues on his running path—with or without the football.

- This phase of the drill continues until all drill participants have had a sufficient number of repetitions.

- Drill should be conducted left and right.

Phase III: The *mesh* phase of the drill combines the *blind set* and *fit* phases of the drill and is designed to give the quarterback and fullback full-speed repetitions in executing the *read key* option.

- The center, quarterback and fullback are all aligned as noted in Phase I.

- The *mesh* phase of the drill is continued until all drill participants have had a sufficient number of repetitions.

- Drill should be conducted both left and right.

Coaching Points:

- During the *blind set* phase of the drill, make sure the quarterbacks and fullbacks are aligned correctly and are in their proper stances. Check to see that the quarterback's feet are under the shoulders, that the fullback's feet are tight together and that the majority of the weight is on the hands and fingers.

- During the *fit* phase of the drill, make sure the quarterback concentrates on both *squeezing* the football and focusing on the *read key*.

- Also during the *fit* phase, instruct the fullback to concentrate on *squeezing* the football and continuing on his running path when he hears the coaches whistle.

- During the *mesh* phase of the drill, emphasize the importance of the quarterback's and the fullback's getting the *feel* for each other and developing the *tempo* of the mesh.

Safety Considerations:

- Proper warm-up should precede drill.

- The drill area should be clear of all foreign articles.

- During the *mesh* phase of the drill, it is imperative that the *read key* defender holds a hand shield in case of collision with the fullback.

Variation:

- Can incorporate a slot back and run the slot back option. When incorporating the slot back option, defenders should be placed at both the *read key* and the *pitch key*.

9

Passing Game Drills

QUICK RELEASE AND SNATCH

Gary Patterson
California Lutheran University, University of California at Davis,
Tennessee Technological University, Pittsburg State University,
Sonoma State University, Oregon Lightning Bolts, Utah State University,
United States Naval Academy, University of New Mexico, Texas Christian University

Objective: To teach and practice the proper mechanics in developing the *quick* release when throwing the football for the quarterbacks and teaching the receivers to *snatch* the football when making the catch.

Equipment Needed: Footballs

Description:

- Position a row of quarterbacks, with footballs in hand, five yards apart on a selected line of scrimmage.

- Position a row of receivers, with hands at their sides, 10 yards in front of and facing the row of quarterbacks.

- The coach stands adjacent to the drill area (see diagram).

- On coach's command, all quarterbacks, from a *squared* stance, go through their normal warm-up procedure using a full extension and proper rotation, and pass the football to their front-facing receiver. The receiver with their hands at their sides reaches up and *snatches* the thrown footballs.

- Quarterbacks now move to a position 15 yards from the receivers, and from their *normal* throwing stance and on coach's command, pass the football to the receivers who are now turned sideways (either left or right) to the quarterback. The receivers again concentrate on *snatching* the thrown pass.

- Quarterbacks now move back to their *squared* stance and 10 yards from the receivers. On coach's command, the quarterbacks pass the footballs to the receivers with emphasis on executing a *quick* release. Receivers are once again facing the quarterbacks with hands at their sides and concentrate on *snatching* the thrown football.

- Drill continues with the quarterbacks positioned in their *normal* stances and 15 yards from the receivers. On coach's command, the quarterbacks pass the football with emphasis again on executing the *quick* release. The receivers are again positioned sideways (either left or right) to the quarterbacks and again concentrate on *snatching* the thrown football.

- The drill continues with the quarterbacks again positioned 15 yards from the receivers and, on coach's first command, the quarterbacks begin walking away from the receivers. On coach's second command, the quarterbacks turn the *easy way*—emphasizing both *quick* feet and the *quick* release. The receivers are now turned with their backs to the quarterbacks. On coach's second command, receivers turn and face the quarterbacks, concentrating on both *quick* feet and *snatching* the football.

- The previous description is repeated with the quarterback turning the *hard way* and passing the football to the receivers.

- Each phase of the drill is continued until all quarterbacks and receivers have had a sufficient number of repetitions.

Coaching Points:

- Make sure all the quarterbacks practice the proper mechanics in throwing all passes.

- Instruct quarterbacks in descriptions six and seven to concentrate on the importance of the *quick* release.

- In descriptions eight and nine, emphasize for the quarterbacks the importance of the feet *beating* their hands.

- Instruct all receivers to concentrate on *looking* every thrown pass into their hands until the football is safely *tucked* away.

- Also for the receivers, stress the importance of relaxing and keeping their hands at their sides before *snatching* the thrown pass.

- In descriptions eight and nine, instruct the receivers to concentrate on both quick feet and *snatching* the football.

Variations:

- Can be used with quarterbacks and receivers positioned at various distances apart.

- Can be used with alternating quarterbacks serving as receivers.

- Can be used as a running back receiving drill.

- Can be used with various quarterback pass drops.

MAXIMUM-PASS DRILL*

Phillip James "Jim" Butterfield (Deceased)
University of Maine, Colgate University, Ithaca College
National Champions: Ithaca 1979, 1988, and 1991
National Coach of the Year: Ithaca 1988 and 1991
College Football Hall of Fame: 1997

Objective: To teach and practice the proper fundamentals and techniques in the execution of various pass patterns.

Equipment Needed: Footballs

Description:

- Align three quarterbacks (A, B, C) under centers at the midpoint of a selected line of scrimmage. A four-foot separation is between the centers.

- Position four receivers at various alignments on the line of scrimmage. Each receiver must be positioned at an appropriate distance relative to the quarterback who will pass him the football and the pattern to be run (see diagram).

- Coaches align themselves as defenders.

- With the middle quarterback designated to call cadence, quarterbacks execute one of three pass drop actions (quarterback A—a three-step quick pass, quarterback B —a play-action pass, and quarterback C—a sprint-out pass).

- Alternating drill participants stand adjacent to the drill area.

- On the cadence and ball snap, the quarterbacks take their designated pass drops and pass the footballs to assigned receivers who have run predetermined pass routes.

- The drill continues until the quarterbacks and receivers have run a sufficient number of varying pass actions and patterns.

- The drill should be conducted from both left and right formations and from various field positions.

Coaching Points:

- Always check to see that all personnel are aligned correctly and are in proper stances.

*Reprinted with permission from 101 Winning Football Drills: From the Legends of the Game by Jerry Tolley

- Instruct the quarterbacks to rotate their positions under the centers after each pass.
- Coaches should present imaginary secondary reads for quarterbacks and receivers.
- Make sure all quarterbacks practice the proper mechanics in throwing all passes.
- Make sure all quarterbacks take their proper pass drop action.
- Instruct all receivers to run all their patterns correctly and with authority.
- Insist that the drill be conducted at full speed.

Safety Considerations:
- Proper warm-up should precede the drill.
- The drill area should be clear of all foreign articles.
- Instruct the receivers to run complementary pass patterns.
- Maintain a minimum distance of four-yards between the three quarterbacks.
- All quarterback pass-drop actions must always be in the same direction.

Variations:
- Can be used with all quarterbacks taking the same pass-drop action.
- Can be used with receivers running a variety of complementing patterns.
- Can be used with coaches or secondary personnel providing reads for quarterbacks.
- Can incorporate offensive backs and run play-action passes.
- Can be used as a secondary drill.

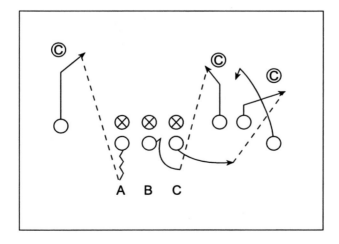

THREE QUARTERBACK DRILL

Terry Hoeppner
Franklin College, Miami University (Ohio), Indiana University
National Coach of the Year: Miami 2003

Objectives: To teach and practice the proper fundamentals and techniques in the execution of various pass patterns. The drill can also be used in installing the passing game.

Equipment Needed: Footballs

Description:

- Align three quarterbacks under centers at the midpoint of a selected line of scrimmage. One yard separates the three centers.

- Alternating quarterbacks stand adjacent to the drill area or may serve as centers.

- Three receivers (tight end, split end, and flanker) take their normal alignments at the appropriate distances relative to the quarterback who will be passing him the football and the pattern to be run (see diagram).

- Other receivers stand adjacent to their drill area.

- The coach is positioned behind the offense and calls out the formation and the pattern to be run.

- On designated quarterback's (middle quarterback's) cadence and snap count, the three quarterbacks take their designated pass drop and pass the football to the assigned receiver who is running the predetermined pass route.

- Drill continues until all quarterbacks and receivers have run a sufficient number of varying pass drop actions and pass patterns.

- Drill should be conducted from both left and right formations and from various field positions.

Coaching Points:

- Always check to see that all personnel are aligned correctly and are in their proper stances.

- Before the cadence is called, make sure each quarterback designates the receiver to whom he will be passing the football.

- Make sure all quarterbacks take their designated pass drop and that receivers drive out of their stance and run the designated pass route with authority.

- Instruct the quarterbacks to go through their appropriate secondary read sequence before throwing their passes. (This exercise will ensure that passes are thrown at different times.)

- Make sure all quarterbacks practice the proper mechanics in throwing all passes.

- Insist that the drill be conducted at full speed.

Safety Considerations:

- Proper warm-up should precede drill.

- Drill area should be clear of all foreign articles.

- To avoid collisions in the backfield, all quarterback pass actions must be in the same direction.

- Insist that the quarterbacks go through their read sequences to ensure that all passes are thrown at different times.

Variation:

- Drill can be used with additional quarterbacks and receivers.

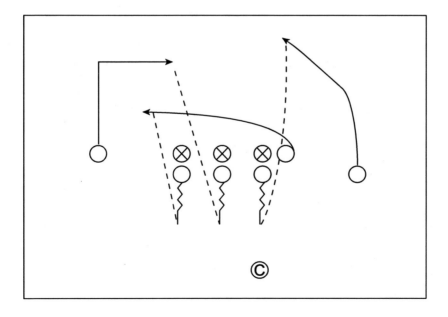

CURL READ*

Larry Kehres
Mount Union College
National Champions: 1993, 1996, 1997, 1998, 2000, and 2001
National Coach of the Year 1993, 1996, 1997, 1998, 2000, and 2001

Objective: To teach and practice the proper mechanics of passing the football and reading the open receiver against a curl/flat defender for quarterbacks; running the correct pass route and catching the football for the receivers.

Equipment Needed: Footballs

Description:

- Align a quarterback and center over the football at the midpoint of a selected line of scrimmage.

- Position twin receivers in their proper curl/flat-pass play relationship to the quarterback.

- Other drill participants stand adjacent to the drill area.

- A defender (coach) is positioned at the curl/flat defender position.

- On the quarterback's cadence and snap count, the receivers run their designated curl/flat-pass routes as the quarterback takes his normal five-step pass drop (see diagram).

- As the quarterback is completing his pass drop, the defender (coach) moves to cover either the curl or flat receiver. (Movement by the coach is only two steps.) The quarterback reads the coverage of the defender (coach) and passes to the open receiver.

- The drill continues until all participants have had a sufficient number of executions.

- The drill should be conducted from various field alignments and from both left and right formations.

Coaching Points:

- Always check to see that all the drill participants are aligned correctly and are in their proper stances.

*Reprinted with permission from 101 Winning Football Drills: From the Legends of the Game by Jerry Tolley

- Instruct the quarterbacks to make their read on the defender (coach) as they take their fifth drop step.

- Insist that the receivers run their curl/flat-pass routes correctly and at full speed.

- Make sure all quarterbacks use proper passing mechanics with each pass thrown.

- Insist that the receivers catch the football with their hands, tuck it away, and sprint for a designated distance.

Safety Considerations:

- Proper warm-up should precede the drill.

- The drill area (including sideline areas) should be cleared of all foreign articles.

- Helmets should be worn and chinstraps snapped.

Variations:

- Can be used with any combination-pass patterns.

- Can be used with a three-receiver pass route utilizing three defenders.

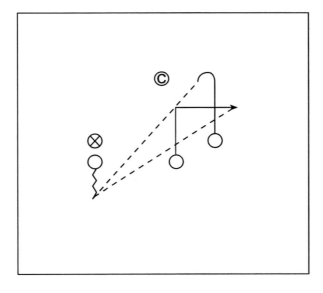

END OF PATTERN DRILL

James E. "Jim" Harkema
Northern Illinois University, Grand Valley State University, Eastern Michigan University

Objective: To teach and practice the proper fundamentals and techniques in the execution of the ending steps of various individual pass routes. Incorporated are skills related to passing and receiving with special emphasis on the receiver depth and the timing of the quarterback's pass.

Equipment Needed: One hand shield and footballs

Description:

- Align a quarterback, holding a football, at a designated pass drop position from a selected line of scrimmage.

- Position a receiver at a point downfield five yards from the completion point of a designated pass pattern.

- A defender, holding a hand shield, is placed near the pass completion point.

- The coach stands behind the quarterback and in a position that allows him to observe both the quarterback and receiver.

- Alternating drill participants stand adjacent to their drill area.

- On quarterback's command, the receiver runs the last five steps of a designated pass pattern and the quarterback sets and throws him the pass. As the receiver makes the catch, the defender *jams* him with the hand shield.

- After each pass is completed, the receiver returns the football to the quarterback and goes to the opposite side of the field and takes a corresponding position five yards from the ending point of the same pass pattern.

- Drill continues with alternating quarterbacks passing to receivers at various pass completion points and from various positions on the field.

Coaching Points:

- The coach should pay special attention to the timing of the quarterbacks' passes.

- Make sure all quarterbacks practice the proper mechanics in throwing all passes.

- Make sure receivers are at proper pass-pattern ending point and that their footwork is executed property.

Safety Considerations:

- Proper warm-up should precede drill.
- Drill area should be clear of all foreign articles.
- Helmets should be worn with chinstraps snapped.
- Instruct the shield holder not to *jam* the receivers in the head area.

Variations:

- Can be used with drill participants running through the entire pattern.
- Can have defender wave the hand shield in front of the pass while it is in flight.

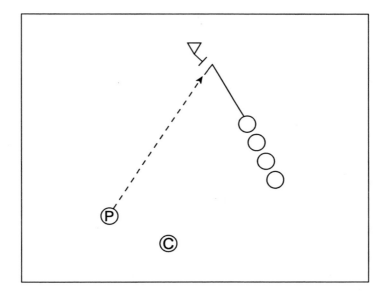

RELAY-LINE DRILL*

Dr. Darrell Eugene Mudra

Huron University, Northern Colorado University, Adams State University,
North Dakota State University, Montreal Alouettes, University of Arizona,
Western Illinois University, Florida State University,
Eastern Illinois University, University of Northern Iowa
National Champions: North Dakota State 1965; Eastern Illinois 1978
College Football Hall of Fame: 2000

Objective: To teach and practice the proper fundamentals and techniques in throwing and catching the football from various receiver-quarterback relationships. Can also be used as a warm-up drill.

Equipment Needed: Footballs

Description:

- Position all receivers and quarterbacks into two groups on selected yard lines as shown in diagram. Twenty yards should separate the two groups.

- Align each group in a receiver-quarterback relationship that allows receiver to make an over-the-shoulder catch as shown in diagram A.

- On quarterback's cadence, the first receiver in each group runs across the field as the respective quarterback passes him the football.

- After the catch is made, each receiver carries the football to the quarterback in the other group and joins that group.

- After all the drill participants have had a sufficient number of repetitions from this alignment, the quarterbacks change their positions to set up a crossing-pattern relationship with receivers (see diagram B).

- The drill continues until all the drill participants have had a sufficient number of repetitions.

Coaching Points:

- Make sure all the quarterbacks practice the proper mechanics in throwing all passes.

- Insist that receivers catch all passes with their hands.

- Instruct receivers to place special emphasis on concentration.

*Reprinted with permission from 101 Winning Football Drills: From the Legends of the Game by Jerry Tolley

Safety Considerations:

- The drill area should be clear of all foreign articles.

- The drill should progress from half speed with short passes to full speed with longer passes.

- Helmets should be worn with chinstraps snapped.

Variations:

- Can be used with quarterback and receivers aligned in a variety of relationships.

- Can be used with receivers running in a counterclockwise direction.

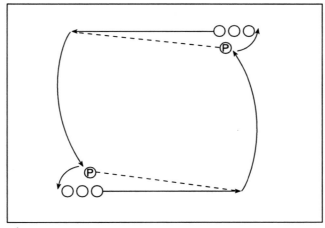

Diagram A

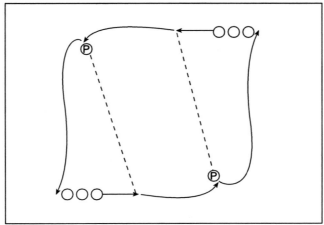

Diagram B

QUARTERBACK READING DRILL

Ernest R. Hawkins
East Texas State University
National Champions: 1972

Objectives: To teach and practice the proper fundamentals and techniques of reading the defense and adjusting the sprint draw pass series according to different secondary coverages.

Equipment Needed: Footballs

Description:

- Align offensive personnel (center, quarterback, tight end, flanker, fullback, and tailback) over the football at the midpoint of a selected line of scrimmage.

- Place defenders at the strong safety and strong corner positions (see diagram).

- Alternating offensive personnel are positioned behind the performing drill participants.

- On quarterback's cadence and ball snap, the offense executes the basic pass play, *flat*, off the sprint draw series. The defenders react with one of three coverages— *man, sky,* or *cloud*.

- Against all coverages, the flanker runs a deep clear out pass pattern as shown in diagrams.

- The tight end (as the primary receiver) varies his pass route according to the secondary coverage. Against *man* and *sky* coverage (diagram A), he tries to head up the strong safety and then breaks outside and toward the line of scrimmage. If the strong safety comes up, the tight end runs behind him angling for a position 15 yards deep. If he cannot get open outside or behind the safety, he hooks. Against *cloud* coverage, the tight end runs a pass route to get open in the seam as shown in diagram B.

- The quarterback reads the secondary as well as the movement of the tight end and throws the pass at the appropriate time.

- Drill continues until all offensive personnel have had a sufficient number of repetitions.

- Drill should be run from both left and right formations and from various field positions.

Coaching Points:

- Always check to see that all personnel are aligned correctly and are in their proper stances.

- Instruct the quarterbacks to read the coverage on their third pass drop step.

- Insist that the backfield personnel execute the sprint draw fake correctly.

- Instruct the tight ends to consider the quarterback's fake and setup as they move to get open.

- Make sure that all quarterbacks practice the proper mechanics in throwing all passes.

Safety Considerations:

- Proper warm-up should precede drill.

- Drill area should be clear of all foreign articles.

- Helmets should be worn with chinstraps snapped.

- Drill should progress from form work to full speed (no tackling).

- Coach should monitor closely the intensity of the drill.

Variations:

- Can be used with a variety of pass patterns.

- Can incorporate other defensive personnel.

- Can be used as a form or full speed drill.

- Can be used as a defensive drill.

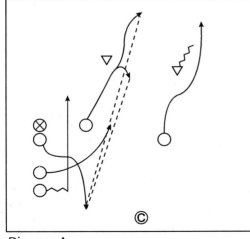

Diagram A

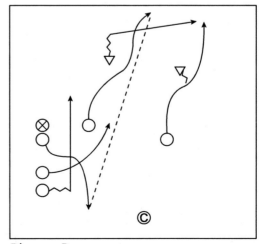

Diagram B

SCRAMBLE DRILL*

John T. Majors
Mississippi State University, University of Arkansas, Iowa State University,
University of Pittsburgh, University of Tennessee
National Champions: Pittsburgh 1976
National Coach of the Year: Pittsburgh 1973 and 1976
AFCA President: 1990

Objective: To teach and practice skills related to scramble-passing and pass- receiving rules. Incorporated are skills related to throwing the football while being chased, finding the open receiver, throwing the ball away if necessary for the quarterback, and redirecting a called pass pattern by the receiver.

Equipment Needed: Footballs

Description:

- Align a skeleton-pass offense over the football at the midpoint of a selected line of scrimmage.

- A perimeter-pass defense is positioned over the offense. Two additional defenders are placed at the defensive guard position.

- Alternating offensive personnel stand adjacent to their drill areas.

- The quarterback instructs all offensive personnel as to the pass pattern to be run using the regular audible system.

- On the cadence and ball snap, the quarterback executes his pass drop as the receivers run their assigned pass routes.

- The defensive-perimeter players react to the offense in any manner they wish. Their goal is to intercept or prevent the reception. The two additional defenders (guards) are instructed to delay their charge until the quarterback has initiated his scramble. They then take chase and tag the quarterback.

- When the quarterback initiates his scramble, the receivers alter their designated pass route and follow their normal scramble rules (see diagram).

- The drill continues until the alternating personnel have had a sufficient number of repetitions.

- The drill should be conducted from both left and right formations and from various field positions.

*Reprinted with permission from 101 Winning Football Drills: From the Legends of the Game by Jerry Tolley

Coaching Points:

- Always check to see that all personnel are aligned correctly and are in their proper stances.

- Make sure all the receivers follow their assigned scramble rules.

- Instruct the quarterbacks to tuck the football and run or throw the pass away if necessary.

- Make sure all the receivers sprint to the football and become blockers after the pass is thrown.

- Insist that the drill be conducted at full speed.

Safety Considerations:

- Proper warm-up is imperative with this drill.

- The drill area (including sideline areas) should be clear of all foreign articles.

- Although the drill is conducted at full speed, the tackling of receivers is not encouraged except under the most monitored conditions.

- The coach should monitor closely the intensity of the drill.

- A quick whistle is imperative with this drill.

Variations:

- Can have the quarterback reverse his field after his initial scramble.

- Can be used as a defensive drill.

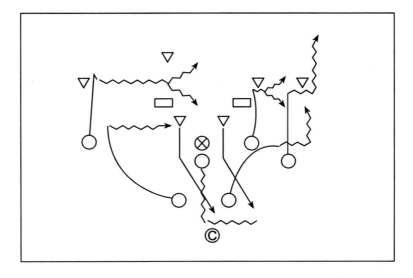

READ AND COVER DRILL

Chuck Mills
Southern Oregon State College, Utah State University, Wake Forest University,
United States Coast Guard Academy, United States Merchant Marine Academy,
Kansas City Chiefs

Objective: To teach and practice the proper fundamentals and techniques in the execution of various two-side receiver pass patterns. Incorporated are skills of reading for the quarterbacks and catching the football for the receivers.

Equipment Needed: Footballs

Description:

- Align paired quarterbacks and centers over footballs at the midpoint of a selected line of scrimmage. Three yards should separate the two centers.

- Position a pair of receivers in various two-side alignments on each side of the quarterback.

- A four-deep secondary is placed over the offense (see diagram).

- The coach is positioned 10 yards behind the quarterback.

- Alternating offensive personnel stand adjacent to their drill area.

- On designated quarterback's cadence and ball snap, both quarterbacks roll toward the onside receivers as the paired receivers run complementing pass patterns.

- Quarterbacks and receivers alike read the secondary (strong safety side and free safety side) and adjust the pass pattern accordingly.

- Drill continues until all alternating offensive personnel have had a sufficient number of repetitions.

- Drill should be run from various field positions.

Coaching Points:

- Always check to see that all personnel are aligned correctly and are in their proper stances.

- Instruct the quarterbacks to rotate their positions under the center after each pass. (Quarterbacks also alternate calling cadence.)

- Make sure all quarterbacks practice the proper mechanics in throwing all passes.

- Quarterbacks should look for their *read key* on the first drop step.
- Instruct all receivers to run their patterns correctly and with authority.

Safety Considerations:
- Proper warm-up should precede drill.
- Drill area should be clear of all foreign articles.
- Helmets should be worn with chinstraps snapped.
- Maintain a minimum distance of three yards between performing centers.

Variations:
- Can incorporate running backs and linebackers.
- Can be used with two strong safeties or two free safeties aligned with cornerbacks.
- Can be used with straight drop back pass action by quarterback.
- Can be used as a defensive secondary drill.

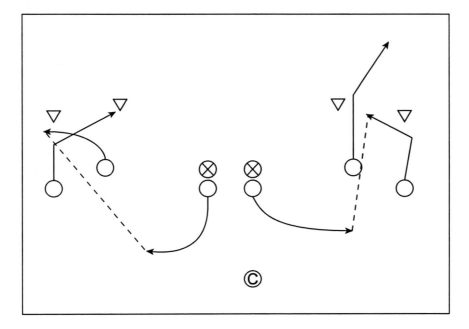

READ SCREEN DRILL

Jim "Red" Parker
University of Arkansas—Monticello, The Citadel, Clemson University, Southern Arkansas University, Delta State University, Ouachita Baptist University, University of Mississippi, Vanderbilt University

Objective: To teach and practice the proper fundamentals and techniques of reading the linebackers in attacking the underneath pass coverage.

Equipment Needed: Footballs

Description:

- Align offensive personnel (center, tackles, tight end, running backs, and quarterback) over the football at the midpoint of a selected line of scrimmage.

- Place two inside linebackers and two defensive tackles over the offense.

- Alternating personnel stand adjacent to drill area.

- The coach is positioned behind the offense and signals the pass routes to be run.

- On designated quarterback's cadence and ball snap, the designated pass receivers run their assigned pass routes as the quarterback takes his designated pass drop, reads the linebackers, avoids the rush of the defensive tackles, and passes the football to the appropriate receiver (see diagram).

- Also on ball snap, the offensive tackles move to their *pass set* positions and block the on rushing tackles.

- Drill continues until alternating personnel have had a sufficient number of repetitions.

- Drill should be run from both left and right formations and from various field positions.

Coaching Points:

- Make sure all drill participants are aligned correctly and are in their proper stances.

- Instruct the quarterbacks to begin their *read* on the first step of their pass drop.

- Insist that all receivers run their pass routes correctly and with authority.

- Make sure all quarterbacks practice the proper mechanics in throwing all passes.

- Check to see that quarterbacks take their proper pass drops.
- Instruct the offensive tackles to maintain good pass block leverage with their defenders.

Safety Considerations:

- It is imperative that proper warm-up precede drill.
- Drill area should be clear of all foreign articles.
- Drill should progress from form work to live work.
- The coach should monitor closely the intensity of the drill.
- Instruct offensive tackles not to cut block the pass rushers.
- A quick whistle is imperative with this drill.
- The training staff should be placed on special alert.

Variations:

- Can be used as either a passive or live drill.
- Can be used with offensive backs blocking blitzing linebackers and ends.
- Can be used with offensive front blocking defensive front.
- Can be used as a defensive drill.

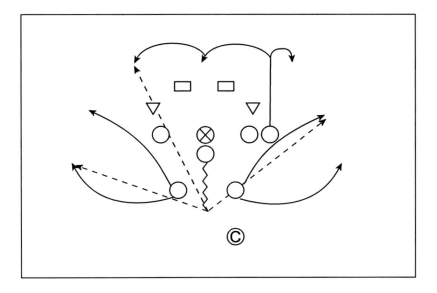

PLAY-ROUTE REPETITION*

Lee J. Tressel (Deceased) [Drill submitted by Dick Tressel] Baldwin-Wallace College National Champions: 1978 National Coach of the Year: 1978 College Football Hall of Fame: 1996

Objective: To teach and practice the proper mechanics of setting up and passing the football for quarterbacks, and running the correct pass route and catching the football for receivers.

Equipment Needed: 10 footballs

Description:

- Select a designated pass play to be used as the *pass play of the day*.

- Align five quarterbacks (with two footballs each) on the hash marks on the right side of the field, and on selected lines of scrimmage as noted in the following bulleted procedures four through eight. (All quarterbacks are positioned on the same side of the field hash marks.) Quarterbacks one, two, and four throw passes toward midfield, while quarterbacks three and five throw passes toward the end zone (see diagram).

- Quarterback number one positions himself on the hash mark of his own goal line and passes the football to the flankers.

- Quarterback number two positions himself on the hash mark of his own 15-yard line and passes the football to the tight ends.

- Quarterback number three positions himself on the hash mark of the opponent's 16-yard line and passes the football to the split ends.

- Quarterback number four positions himself on the hash mark of his own 35-yard line and passes the football to the strongside running backs.

- Quarterback number five positions himself on the hash mark on the opponent's 36-yard line and passes the football to the weakside running backs.

- On the individual quarterback's cadence and snap count, receivers run their designated *pass-play-of-the-day* pass routes as quarterbacks execute their correct pass drops. Each quarterback throws two passes from each field alignment and

*Reprinted with permission from *101 Winning Football Drills: From the Legends of the Game* by Jerry Tolley

then moves upfield to the next field alignment. The quarterback passing to the weakside running backs proceeds to the goal line.

- All the receivers remain at the same field alignment throughout the drill. They are also responsible for returning the footballs to the quarterback at their station.

- After each quarterback has thrown two passes from each field alignment, the passing field is reversed and quarterbacks and receivers move to the opposite hash mark and the drill continues.

Coaching Points:

- Always check to see that all the drill participants are aligned correctly and are in their proper stances.

- Stress the importance of running all pass routes correctly and at full speed.

- Instruct all quarterbacks to follow their read progression with every pass. (Each quarterback will assume a specific coverage before calling the cadence.)

- Make sure the quarterbacks take the correct pass drop and use proper passing mechanics with each thrown pass.

- Insist that the quarterbacks hustle as they move from one station to another and that the receivers sprint downfield after each catch and hustle as they return the ball to the quarterback.

Safety Considerations:

- Proper warm-up should precede the drill.

- The drill area (including sideline areas) should be clear of all foreign objects.

- Insist that alternating pass receivers remain alert and align themselves in a safe position as pass patterns are being thrown.

- In assigning receivers to each station, the coach much be fully aware of each pass route to be run and the field allotment needed.

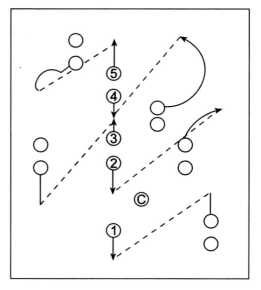

READING TEST FOR QUARTERBACKS

Dwight D. Wallace
Iowa Wesleyan College, Central Michigan University, University of Colorado,
Ball State University, West Virginia University

Objective: To teach and practice the proper fundamentals and techniques in reading various defenses.

Equipment Needed: Footballs

Description:

- Align a skeleton pass offense (quarterback, center, running backs, tight end, flanker, and split end) over the football at the midpoint of a selected line of scrimmage (see diagram).

- Alternating offenses stand adjacent to their drill area.

- The coach is positioned behind the offense.

- At the instructions of the coach, all receivers jog to their respective pass completion positions of a designated pass play.

- The coach directs the quarterback as to the *ghost* coverage or linebacker drop. He can also give the quarterback information regarding the particular pass pattern called.

- On cadence and ball snap, the quarterback executes his pass drop and throws the football to the appropriate receiver. The receiver catches the football and turns and sprints up field.

- As the quarterback executes his pass drop, the coach may call, "No! No!" which directs the quarterback to pass the ball to an outlet receiver.

- The coach can also call *scramble*, which directs the quarterback to change his pass drop. When *scramble* is called, all receivers follow their normal *scramble* rules.

- Drill continues until alternating personnel have had a sufficient number of repetitions.

- Drill should be run from both left and right formations and from various field positions.

Coaching Points:

- Make sure all receivers are aligned in their proper pass completion positions for the particular play called.

- Make sure quarterbacks understand the coach's instructions regarding the particular *ghost* coverage and linebacker drop.

- Check to see that quarterbacks take their proper pass drops and read the *ghost* coverage correctly.

- Make sure that all quarterbacks practice the proper mechanics in throwing all passes.

- Insist that receivers sprint up field after each reception.

Safety Considerations:

- Proper warm-up should precede drill.

- Drill area should be clear of all foreign articles.

- Helmets should be worn with chinstraps snapped.

Variations:

- Can be used with a variety of formations, pass drops, and patterns.

- Can incorporate defensive personnel in selected coverages.

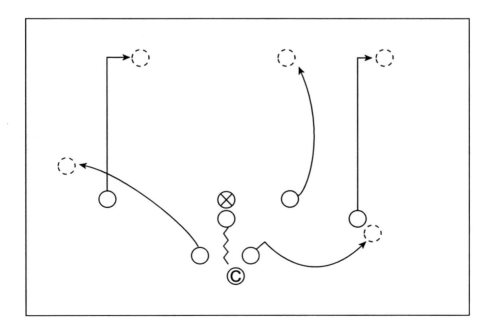

SUPERMARKET DRILL

Dick B. Lowry
Wayne State University, Akron University, Hillsdale College
National Champions: Hillsdale 1985
National Coach of the Year: Hillsdale 1982

Objective: To teach and practice the proper fundamentals and techniques in the execution of all individual pass patterns from a slot formation.

Equipment Needed: Footballs

Description:

- Position a split end, a tight end, and a slot-back in their normal alignments on a selected line of scrimmage.

- Position two quarterbacks, holding footballs, in the middle of the formation. Four yards separate the two quarterbacks. Running backs are aligned in their regular positions (see diagram).

- Alternating drill participants stand adjacent to the drill area.

- At the instructions of the quarterbacks, receivers are directed as to the individual pass pattern they will run. Only one receiver on each side of the offense will run a pattern on each snap.

- On designated quarterback's cadence and snap count, both quarterbacks take their regular pass drop and passes the football to the designated receiver on their side of the field who is running the assigned pass pattern.

- Drill continues until alternating personnel have had a sufficient number of repetitions. Quarterbacks should rotate their passes between slot-back and tight end sides.

- Drill should be conducted from both left and right formations and from various positions on the field.

Coaching Points:

- Always check to see that all personnel are aligned correctly and are in their proper stances.

- Insist that all receivers execute their individual pass patterns correctly.

- Make sure quarterbacks execute their pass drops correctly.

- Make sure all quarterbacks practice the proper mechanics in throwing all passes.

- Insist that the drill be conducted at full speed.

Safety Considerations:

- Proper warm-up should precede drill.

- Drill area should be clear of all foreign articles.

- Drill should be monitored closely to ensure that receivers do not run pass routes that take them into a collision situation.

- Maintain a minimum distance of four yards between quarterbacks.

- Helmets should be worn with chinstraps snapped.

Variations:

- Can be used with various formations and quarterback pass drops.

- Can incorporate defensive secondary personnel.

- Can be used as a defensive secondary drill.

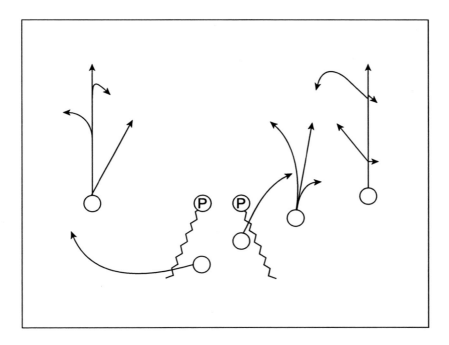

Appendices

Appendix A

Sports Medicine Guidelines*

Dr. Fred Mueller
University of North Carolina-Chapel Hill

Dr. Fred Mueller is Professor and Chairman of the Department of Exercise and Sport Science at The University of North Carolina at Chapel Hill. He currently serves as Director of the National Center for Catastrophic Sports Injury Research at UNC and is Chairman of the American Football Coaches Association Committee on Football Injuries. He is also a member of the American College of Sports Medicine. The following are his recommendations to help reduce football injuries and make the game safer for the participants.

Medical Exam

Mandatory medical examinations and medical history should be taken before allowing an athlete to participate in football. The National Collegiate Athletic Association recommends a thorough medical examination when the athlete first enters the college athletic program and an annual health-history update with use of referral exams when warranted. If the physician or coach has any questions about the athletes' readiness to participate, the athlete should not be allowed to play. High school coaches should follow the recommendations set by their state high school athletic association.

Health Insurance

Each student athlete should be covered by individual, parental, or institutional medical insurance to defray the costs of significant injury or illness. At the high school level, the schools should provide information about association-provided medical insurance.

Preseason Conditioning

All personnel concerned with training football athletes should emphasize proper, gradual, and complete physical conditioning. Special emphasis should be placed on working in hot and humid weather conditions. Recommendations are as follows:

- Athletes must have a physical examination with a history of previous heat illness and type of training activities before organized practice begins.

- Acclimate athletes to heat gradually by providing graduated practice sessions for the first 7 to 10 days and other abnormally hot or humid days.

- Know both the temperature and humidity since it is more difficult for the body to cool itself in high humidity. The use of a sling psychrometer is recommended to measure the relative humidity and anytime the wet-bulb temperature is over 78 degrees practice should be altered.

- Adjust activity levels and provide frequent rest periods. Rest in cool, shaded areas with some air movement and remove helmets and loosen or remove jerseys. Rest periods of 15 to 30 minutes should be provided during workouts of one hour.

- Provide adequate cold water replacement during practice. *Water should always be available and in unlimited quantities to the athletes—give water regularly.*

- Salt should be replaced daily and a liberal salting of the athletes' food will accomplish this purpose. Coaches should not give salt tablets to athletes. Attention must be given to water replacement.

- Athletes should weigh each day before and after practice. Weight charts should be checked each day in order to treat athletes who lose excessive weight.

- Clothing is important and a player should avoid using long sleeves and any excess clothing. Never use rubberized clothing or sweat suits.

- Some athletes are more susceptible to heat injury than others. These individuals are not accustomed to working out in the heat, may be overweight, or may be the eager athlete who constantly competes at his capacity. Athletes with previous heat problems should be watched closely.

- It is important to observe for signs of heat illness. Some trouble signs are nausea, incoherence, fatigue, weakness, vomiting, weak rapid pulse, flushed appearance, visual disturbance, and unsteadiness. If heat illness is suspected, seek a physician's immediate service.

Facilities

It is the responsibility of the school administration to provide excellent facilities for the athletic program. The coach must monitor these facilities and keep them in the best condition.

Emergency Procedures

Each institution should strive to have a certified athletic trainer who is also a member of the school faculty. A team physician should be available for all games and readily available in other situations. There should also be a written emergency-procedure plan in place for catastrophic or serious injuries. All of the trainers and coaches should be familiar with the emergency plan.

Head and Neck Injuries

Coaches should continue to teach and emphasize the proper fundamentals of blocking and tackling to help reduce head and neck injuries. When a player has experienced or shown signs of head trauma (loss of consciousness, visual disturbances, headache, inability to walk correctly, obvious disorientation, memory loss), he should receive immediate medical attention and should not be allowed to return to practice or a game without permission from the proper medical authorities.

Records

Adequate and complete records of each injury should be kept and analyzed to determine injury patterns and to make recommendations for prevention.

Final Recommendations

- Strict enforcement of the rules of the game by both coaches and officials will help reduce injuries.
- You must keep the head out of blocking and tackling. *Keep the head out of football.*
- There should be a renewed emphasis on employing well-trained athletic personnel, providing excellent facilities, and securing the safest and best equipment available.

---

* Reprinted with permission from *101 Winning Football Drills: From the Legends of the Game* by Jerry Tolley

Appendix B

Medical and Legal Considerations*

Dr. Herb Appenzeller
Guilford College

Dr. Herb Appenzeller is a former athletics director at Guilford College and Professor of Sports Management Emeritus. He is also a former football coach. He has authored and edited 16 books in the area of sport law, risk management, and sport management. He is the co-editor of *From The Gym To The Jury*, a sport-law newsletter. He is a member of four sports Halls of Fame. At the present, he is Executive-in-Residence in graduate Sport Administration at Appalachian State University.

No one wants an athlete to be injured. In sports activities, however, there is always the possibility of injury no matter how careful you are in observing proper procedures. And no one wants to be involved in a lawsuit. Today we have an unprecedented number of sports-related litigation that concerns everyone associated with sports.

The fact that injury occurs does not necessarily mean that the coach is negligent or liable for damages. No sure criteria exist for determining what is negligent action since each case stands individually on its own merit. The following recommendations can help prevent situations that may lead to injuries or litigation:

- Require a thorough physical examination before the athlete engages in the sport.
- Assign someone to make certain all equipment fits properly.
- Assign someone to inspect equipment for defects and the facilities for hazards. Keep an accurate record of each inspection.
- Obtain medical insurance coverage for the athlete and liability insurance for the coaches and other staff members.
- Adopt a medical plan for emergency treatment for all athletes involved in physical contact or strenuous exercise.
- Assign drills within the athlete's range of ability and commensurate with his size, skill, and physical condition.
- Prepare the athlete gradually for all physical drills and progress from simple to complex tasks in strenuous and dangerous drills.

- Warn the athlete of all possible dangers inherent in the drills in which he is involved.
- Follow the activities as designed. If the coach deviates from the prescribed drills, the decision to do so should be based on sound reasoning. Extra precautions for safety should be taken.
- Adopt a policy regarding injuries. Do not attempt to be a medical specialist in judging the physical condition of an athlete under your care.
- Require a physician's medical permission before permitting seriously injured or ill athletes to return to normal practice.
- Avoid moving the injured athlete until it is safe to do so. Whenever the athlete is moved, make certain he is taken away from potentially dangerous playing areas.
- Conduct periodic medical/legal in-service training programs for all personnel.

Risk management has become a vital part of the overall athletics program and football coaches should develop risk management strategies as they relate to their use of drills such as:

- Avoid terminology such as *suicide drills, death run, and hamburger drill.* These terms could come back to haunt you in court.
- In the event of an injury, always follow up with a call or visit to check on the athlete's condition. However, never, never admit fault or assign blame.
- Isolate and keep under lock and key equipment involved in a serious injury (helmet, protective pads, etc.).
- Be aware that you can be sued, but don't panic. Be prepared and coach with confidence.

* Reprinted with permission from *101 Winning Football Drills: From the Legends of the Game* by Jerry Tolley

Appendix C

Summer Two-A-Day Practice Guidelines*

The American Football Coaches Association and the National Athletic Trainers' Association have launched a new educational initiative, HEAT (Helping Educate Athletes in Training). The program is designed to help coaches better prepare their athletes for the grueling conditions of two-a-day practices.

These two-a-day workouts allow for accelerated physical conditioning, increased strength training, and skill development, and can even help develop bonds between teammates. But because these workouts usually occur in hot summer months, heat-related stress becomes a serious concern. Studies have shown that football players can lose dangerously high levels of fluid in 24 hours during two-a-day workouts. Additionally, athletes who are not properly acclimatized to the heat are highly susceptible to injury.

Tips for Safer Two-A-Days

Injury rates increase during two-a-day workouts whether athletes are in peak physical condition or not. In fact, many athletes don't even make their starting lineup because of injuries incurred during preseason training. The following tips can help ensure that athletes stay at their best and prevent heat-related injuries during two-a-days.

Encourage Athletes to Begin Conditioning Before Two-A-Days

Encourage athletes to begin conditioning in the heat two weeks before official practice begins. This allows their bodies to cool more efficiently by increasing sweat production sooner than when they are not acclimated to the heat.

Avoid Workouts During Unusually Hot Temperature

Practice sessions during unusually hot and humid conditions should be limited to very moderate workouts, postponed until cooler time of the day, or brought inside to avoid the heat.

Make Fluids Part of the Playbook

Before, during, and after competition, be sure to consume adequate amounts of fluid. Athletes can make sure they are properly hydrated by checking their urine color: lighter

*Printed with the permission of the **AFCA** and the **NATA** from their summer **HEAT** publication.*

urine color indicates athletes are better hydrated. The longer the workout session, the more frequently fluids need to be replaced. Research shows that a sports drink containing a six percent carbohydrate solution, like Gatorade, can be absorbed as rapidly as water. But unlike water, a sports drink can provide energy, delay fatigue, and improve performance.

Use the Shade

Before practice, warm up in the shade and be sure to rest in the shade during breaks. Even during rest, exposure to heat can raise the body temperature, increase fluid loss, and decrease the blood available to the muscles during workouts.

Recommend Wearing Loose Fitting Clothing

Cotton blend, loose fitting clothing can help promote heat loss. The rule: the less clothing, the better.

Be Prepared for an Emergency

Always have a cell phone on hand and be familiar with emergency numbers. Also keep ice and ice towels on hand in case of heat-related emergencies.

Fluids Guidelines for Two-A-Days

Proper hydration is the best safeguard against heat illness. Remember to have athletes drink before, during, and after training and competition. The following fluid consumption guidelines can help safeguard athletes against heat-related illness.

Before Exercise

- Two to three hours before exercise drink at least 17 to 20 oz. of water or sports drink.
- Ten to twenty minutes before exercise drink another 7 to 10 oz. of water or sports drink.

What to Drink During Exercise

- Drink early—even minimal dehydration compromises performance. In general, every 10 to 20 minutes drink at least 7 to 10 oz. of water or sports drink. To maintain hydration remember to drink beyond thirst. Optimally, drink fluids based on amount of heat and urine loss.
- Athletes benefit in many situations from drinking a sports drink containing carbohydrate.
- If exercise lasts more than 45 to 50 minutes or is intense, a sports drink should be provided during the session.

- The carbohydrate concentration in the ideal fluid replacement solution should be in the range of six to eight percent (14 g/8 oz.).
- During events when a high rate of fluid intake is necessary to sustain hydration, sport drink with less than seven percent carbohydrate should be used to optimize delivery.
- Fluids with salt (sodium chloride) are beneficial to increasing thirst and voluntary fluid intake as well as offsetting the amount in lost sweat.
- Cool beverages at temperatures of 50 to 59 degrees Fahrenheit are recommended.

What Not to Drink During Exercise

- Fruit juices, carbohydrate gels, sodas, and those sports drinks that have carbohydrate levels greater than 8% area not recommended as the sole beverage.
- Beverages containing caffeine, alcohol, and carbonation are discouraged during exercises because they can dehydrate the body by stimulating excess urine production, or decrease voluntary fluid intake.

After Exercises

Immediately after training or competition is the key time to replace fluids. Weigh athletes before and after exercise. Research indicates that for every pound of weight lost, athletes should drink at least 20 oz. of fluid to optimize rehydration. Sports beverages are an excellent choice.

About the Author

Jerry R. Tolley is the former head football coach at Elon University. Under his leadership, Elon earned a 49-11-2 record, claiming consecutive national titles in 1980 and 1981. His 1977 and 1978 squads were nationally ranked number six and number two, respectively. During his five-year head-coaching career, his teams garnered an 8-1 record in playoff bowl competition and won an impressive 80.6 % of all games played.

During his career, Tolley received numerous coaching honors, including conference, district, state, area, and national coach of the year awards. In January 2003, he received the lifetime membership award from the American Football Coaches Association and in June of 2003 received the Johnny Vaught Lifetime Achievement Award from the All-American Football Foundation. He has also received the National Football Foundation Hall of Fame Dwight D. Eisenhower award as well as the State of North Carolina Order of the Long Leaf Pine Award and the Laurel Wreath Award, the highest award given by the State of North Carolina in the area of sports and athletics. Tolley is also a member of Omicron Delta Kappa, the national leadership fraternity.

Tolley is listed in numerous Who's Who volumes, including Marquis Who's Who in America, in the World, in the South and Southwest, in Business and Finance, and in Science and Engineering. He is also listed in *Who's Who among Community Leaders in America, Who's Who in Government Services*, and *Who's Who among World Intellectuals*.

Dr. Tolley's first book, *The American Football Coaches Guide Book To Championship Football Drills*, was published in 1984. His second book, *101 Winning Football Drills: From the Legends of the Game*, was released in 2003 and his third, *The Complete Book of Defensive Football Drills*, followed in 2005. He has also written numerous football-related articles for *Coach and Athlete, The Athletic Journal, The Coaching Clinic*, and the *Journal of Health Physical Education, Recreation, and Dance*. His doctoral dissertation was "The History of Intercollegiate Athletics for Men at Elon College."

Since his retirement from coaching, Dr. Tolley continues to serve Elon University as the director of annual giving. He is also involved in a number of community activities, having served two terms as mayor of the town of Elon, as well as on many local boards, including The Alamance Foundation, The Thomas E. Powell Jr. Biology Foundation, The Community Foundation of Greater Greensboro, The Alamance Education Alliance, and BEACTIVE North Carolina.